D1305512

GLORIOUS
Flowers

GLORIOUS
Flowers

❧ ARRANGING FOR EVERY OCCASION ❧

DEREK AND CAROLYN FELL

PHOTOGRAPHY BY DEREK FELL

FRIEDMAN/FAIRFAX
PUBLISHERS

A FRIEDMAN/FAIRFAX BOOK

© 1996 by Michael Friedman Publishing Group, Inc.

All rights reserved. No part of this publication may be reproduced, stored in a retrieval system, or transmitted, in any form or by any means, electronic, mechanical, photocopying, recording, or otherwise, without prior written permission from the publisher.

Library of Congress Cataloging-in-Publication data available upon request.

ISBN 1-56799-365-6

Editor: Susan Lauzau
Art Director: Lynne Yeamans
Designer: Andrea Karman
Photography Director: Christopher C. Bain
Production Director: Karen Matsu Greenberg

Color separations by Bright Arts Graphics (S) Pte, Ltd.
Printed in the United Kingdom by Butler & Tanner, Ltd.

For bulk purchases and special sales, please contact:
Friedman/Fairfax Publishers
Attention: Sales Department
15 West 26th Street
New York, New York 10010
212/685-6610   FAX 212/685-1307

Visit the Friedman/Fairfax Website:
http://www.webcom.com/friedman

DEDICATION

For Anna, mother of Carolyn

ACKNOWLEDGMENTS

We owe special thanks to Kathy Nelson, who maintains the farm office

and photo library at Cedaridge Farm, and also to Wendy Fields, grounds supervisor, who helps

maintain the more than twenty theme gardens for thousands of visitors to enjoy.

The wedding arrangements featured in the book were designed for the marriages of Christina

Fell and Timothy Muth, who were married in the gazebo at Cedaridge Farm; and Laura Little

and Christopher Monica, who were married at the nearby Tinicum United Church of Christ.

Also, we are grateful for a pinch of inspiration from the work of Olive Dunn, retired professional

floral arranger, who maintains a picture-perfect cottage garden in New Zealand.

hether we arrange flowers for our own personal enjoyment or for appreciation by others, and whether we design for pleasure or profit, there are some common aesthetic guidelines that truly make flower arranging an art form. Style and creative content play important roles in the ultimate success of an arrangement—that is, its ability to fit into the surroundings and its appropriateness for the occasion, as well as its appeal to the people who view it.

WHAT IS AN ARRANGEMENT
OF FLOWERS?

The accepted definition for a flower arrangement is "a collection of flowers gathered together and placed in a receptacle that will hold water necessary to keep flowers fresh." This description covers a very broad spectrum of designs—from a single rose in a Victorian bud vase to an elaborate composition that celebrates a special event. Births, weddings, and anniversaries as well as civic, religious, and political events are all celebrated using the common language of flowers. Sympathy for a loss and get-well wishes, too, are effectively conveyed with a simple bouquet. These milestones form the framework of our lives, and for centuries flowers have been a means for expressing our deepest emotions.

And arranging flowers gives us an outlet for creativity that goes far beyond the traditional centerpiece. At Cedaridge Farm, our home in Bucks County, Pennsylvania, we are continually looking for new ways to explore the wonders of light and to express mood, activity, or function by grouping flowers and branches beyond the confines of a container. Rather than limiting ourselves to cut flowers, we make good use of all the plants found on our property—bark from beautiful exfoliating trees like river birch; mosses and lichens; paddle-shaped leaves like those of lustrous hostas; and the leathery, serrated leaves of Lenten roses, one of our favorite plants. Vines such as sweet autumn clematis and annual morning glory are intertwined around our dining room chandelier, and iris pods and the starburst flower heads of dill are bunched together with puffy blue hydrangeas on our fireplace mantels.

The container chosen to hold flowers is of paramount importance, and we like to comb flea markets, yard sales, and auctions for unusual and innovative containers. Above all, arranging flowers is an exercise in creative expression, an exercise we like to practice every day of the year in one form or another, often in collaboration.

This book focuses more on the "natural" school of flower arranging than on the modern or line styles (which are tall and sparse) such as ikebana—a Japanese word that means "living flowers." We prefer our arrangements to say "country," for we live in the country and it is the country feeling that most people cherish, even if they happen to live in a busy city.

Far left: Derek gathers summer flowers from one of the cutting gardens at Cedaridge Farm. Left: Carolyn holds bunches of freshly cut daffodils collected from our naturalized plantings.

FLOWERS IN OUR LIVES

Although much inspiration can be drawn from those flower arrangers who have gone before us, it is our individual lifestyles and our responses to the visual world around us that ultimately decide the floral designs that most appeal to us.

Trends in flower arranging—like those in fashion, food, cars, and political and religious expressions—are cyclical and tend to repeat themselves, with slight changes, from one period to another. Sometimes a given style returns to popularity after a few years; other times a particular fashion won't reappear for decades. As we approach the twenty-first century, the struggle between work and leisure time dictates much of our lives and affects the choices we make about expressing ourselves in our surroundings. Some surveys say we have both more spendable income and more leisure time, but it seems we work harder to acquire this income. There are also wider options for the ways we use our leisure time. Perhaps more than at any other time in history, we've come to appreciate a more relaxed, less structured, less demanding way of life. Thus, flower arranging is reaching new heights of interest, touching the lives of everyone—including men.

At Cedaridge Farm, we seek to create for ourselves and our children an understanding of the natural world. We do all that we can to surround ourselves daily with the beauty and bounty of nature. This reflects in our work and also in our home. As we work in our theme gardens—be it the cottage garden, which becomes a sea of color during the growing season, or our productive vegetable garden, which bursts with choice varieties—we are always conscious of the desire for stimulating color, shape, form, and texture, and we are obsessed with bringing indoors as much of the garden world as possible. Throughout the year, our garden helps us express our creativity both indoors and out through the wonderful experience of arranging flowers.

Carolyn and Derek Fell
Cedaridge Farm
Bucks County, Pennsylvania

CHAPTER 1

Inspiration

"You need a certain dose of inspiration…

in order to do beautiful things."

Vincent van Gogh

in a letter to his brother Theo

Perhaps nothing in the world of flowers is more pleasurable to arrange than sunflowers, a favorite subject of the Impressionist painter Vincent van Gogh. We created this design using his painting "Vase with Twelve Sunflowers" as a starting point.

A bushel basket makes an ideal container for this informal summer bouquet of annuals. Many annuals make good cutting flowers because cutting the blooms actually stimulates the plant to produce more flower buds.

To gain inspiration for floral designs, it is useful to look first at flower arranging in a historical context. Insights into the way people have used flowers through the ages have been provided by archaeologists studying wall decorations and ancient scrolls and by art historians interpreting paintings and, more recently, archive photographs. From our contemporary vantage point, it is fascinating to note the use and specific style of floral arrangements for different periods of history, especially with respect to the use of flowers to celebrate social events, the enhancement of interior design, color preferences through the ages, and specific flower-arranging styles. These historical references show us that the style of expression has changed from one era to another, though the reasons for arranging flowers remain basically the same—to decorate our surroundings and to celebrate life. Flowers have touched every generation and every culture since the beginning of recorded history and continue today to be an important part of our lives, both visually and emotionally.

FLOWERS THROUGHOUT HISTORY

The development of form and style in ancient times provides a strong foundation from which to explore new possibilities and widen our horizons. Ancient Egypt, for instance, was a cultured civilization rich in the use of floral displays. The excavation of tombs reveals the importance of flowers in every part of daily life during that time. Clearly, flowers were used in religious ceremonies, as lavish table decorations, and for personal adornment. By examining jewelry, wall paintings, and pottery, we can identify specific flowers such as lilies, narcissus, jasmine, water lilies, lotuses, roses, violets, and poppies. We can also see that various nonflowering plants—such as figs, citrus fruits, lotus pods, and papyrus—were used as decorative symbols of health, wealth, and fertility. Opulent baskets of fruits, nuts, and berries adorned banquet tables. Many of the containers the Egyptians used, whether made of glass, pottery, or bronze, were in the pedestal style, with fruit piled high and cascading over the edge in a striking show of nature's bounty.

The ancient Greeks favored garlands of grape and laurel leaves as signs of victory, placing these wreaths on the heads of living heroes as well as on statues of gods and goddesses. In ancient Rome, garlands were also used as symbols of honor. Roses, especially those with fragrant petals, were strewn around baths to scent the air and were used like confetti in processions. Banquet tables were traditionally decorated with brightly colored fruits and fragrant flower garlands. A rare Roman mosaic depicts a basket of flowers in an arrangement we might use even today as a centerpiece.

Artwork in the ancient churches of Ravenna, located in modern-day Italy, shows that the Byzantine influence may be responsible for symmetrical, cone-shaped arrangements; these Christmas tree–like decorations featured dried flowers arranged upon a preformed cone.

The influence of Persian flower design is reflected in four bouquets, each made up of a single flower variety. The bold but sophisticated colors are another contribution from the Middle East.

Many expressions in the Byzantine era were geometric; tall, vertical, columnar formations were among the most popular.

Studies of floral design in Persia during the 1300s show a reverence for containers, possibly due to the Oriental influence that followed the advent of trade with China. Short-stemmed blossoms were commonly mounded in symmetrical balance, accented by taller-stemmed blooms such as irises, lilies, or roses, which towered above the mass. Also a significant element in Persian design was the grouping of one flower type or the use of a single flowering shrub cut to form an instant bouquet. Not only were Persian containers more elaborate than those used earlier; the colors were more varied and sophisticated and possibly were influenced by the intricate patterns used in Persian carpets.

Europe's Middle Ages offer little in terms of inspiration for floral artists. There are, however, paintings that display tall, slender vases that hold a few arching stems of one flower form (most often the Madonna lily, which conveyed purity); these arrangements were mainly used in places of worship.

The Renaissance signaled a rebirth of all of the arts, particularly painting and architecture, and with this awakening of artistic sensibilities came a more stylized form of floral display. Formal arrangements that aspired to perfect symmetry became popular and were used far more extensively than the massive banquet table arrangements and simple religious floral decorations of the past. Colors were bright and lively, though apparently selected without regard for pleasing color harmonies. Decorative foliage, fruits and berries, and nuts all added excite-

Compositions of trailing vines and fanciful flowers in delicate shades are reminders of the Rococo period, when such designs first gained popularity. This double heart wall hanging woven with asters, roses, and sweet autumn clematis successfully evokes the playful quality of Rococo arrangements.

ment to Renaissance floral displays. Containers worthy of these opulent arrangements were constructed of a variety of precious metals, and graceful vases of costly Venetian glass brimmed with elegant arching sprays of lilies and roses. Another new development in this period was the creation of small, tight, formal bouquets, similar to late Victorian posies.

The work of Michelangelo greatly influenced the artists and architects of the Baroque period. Extravagant decor, coupled with lavish furnishings, brought about the popularity of bold-colored flowers like ranunculus and anemones, which were displayed in grand profusion. Rhythm and movement dominate these designs, which show an awareness of asymmetrical balance.

Although the Rococo period is often considered an extension of the lavish Baroque period, there were a few distinct developments in flower arranging during this time. The reign of Louis XV of France marked a trend in floral art toward more delicate color and lighthearted, asymmetrical designs. These arrangements often incorporated nonorganic objects such as scrolls, ornate books, and figurines of flora and fauna. Often, the massive floral displays evoked images of ladies in fine silk brocades, billowing petticoats, and flowing skirts, rendered in large, showy blooms finessed with trailing vines of morning glory and honeysuckle. Chinese art, screens, and lacquered porcelain increased in popularity during this time, and the chrysanthemum—a symbol of the Orient—was used with enthusiasm.

Seventeenth-century Dutch and Flemish masters such as Jan van Eyck, Jan van Os, and Jacob von Walscapelli drew from botanical references to paint exuberant, brightly colored bouquets that featured flowers from different seasons and various parts of the world. Insects and branches laden with fruit were portrayed in as much detail as the exotic tulips, poppies, and other garden flowers. The charm of these loose, freely styled, asymmetrical mixed arrangements depends upon the contents rather than on the style of arrangement.

Lace curtains and pretty floral wallpaper in a child's bedroom at Cedaridge Farm inspired this lush Victorian-style arrangement of roses.

By the middle of the nineteenth century, the world had radically changed. A relatively quiet, slow-paced, agrarian culture had metamorphosed into a fast-paced society caught in a whirl-wind of industrial innovation. The population, which had exploded along with the growing economy, gravitated toward cities.

In England, the British welcomed Queen Victoria, and her reign marked a new interest in frills and velvet, deep colors, and romantic notions. Fresh flower arrangements overflowed with roses, tulips, anemones, bleeding hearts, asters, fuchsias, dahlias, pansies, and other newly hybridized cut flowers grown in another product of the industrial revolution—the greenhouse. To break the tightness of designs, plants such as bleeding hearts, ferns, and weeping willow boughs came into vogue; these were useful for draping over the edges of heavy containers. And in the Victorian period, women learned the benefits of dried flower arrangements, protecting their brittleness with glass domes called bell jars. At social gatherings, women liked to carry small clutches of flowers—known as tussie-mussies—made mostly of fragrant flowers such as lavender, sweet violets, and miniature roses and decorated with pieces of lace and ribbon.

This Victorian-style line-mass floral arrangement composed of peonies, foxgloves, and multiflora roses brightens a Victorian-style gazebo at Cedaridge Farm. The combination of the ornate Oriental vase and the flowery French tablecloth contributes to the Victorian motif.

Although the types of flowers changed, we see the massed, opulent arrangement style of the Flemish painters embraced in the Victorian era. As in the seventeenth century, containers again became focal points, with pedestals holding urns of flowers high so that they could literally overflow with blooms. When such attention is paid to the vessel, accord between container and contents becomes vital. Also, the relationship between the arrangement and its placement became critical—an arrangement for a bedroom demanded a different design discipline than a display intended for a foyer. Victorians in England and the United States had little appreciation of color harmony, which would not become an important factor in arranging flowers until the Impressionists' influence came to be felt.

Toward the end of the nineteenth century, architects and designers found themselves in revolt against what they considered the fussiness and overdecoration of High Victorian style. Simplicity, demonstrated by clean, functional lines, became the prevailing notion, and harmonious marriages between natural and man-made forms were emphasized. The preachings of the Shakers in New York State, who were known for their industriousness and their simple way of life, and the increased popularity of the Arts and Crafts movement, which stressed economy of design, created an awareness of minimalism.

The paintings of the Impressionists provide us with much of our inspiration. This arrangement, created in the studio of Pierre-Auguste Renoir at Cagnes-sur-Mer, celebrates the beauty of the gardens there.

Though inspiration for effective color combinations can come from many sources—the fabrics of primitive cultures; the markings of birds, butterflies, and seashells; even the coloration of sunrises and sunsets—our greatest inspiration at Cedaridge Farm has been the Impressionist painters, as well as those who continued their work in the Postimpressionist period. We are particularly drawn to the garden scenes and still-life paintings of Pierre-Auguste Renoir, Claude Monet, Vincent van Gogh, and Paul Cézanne.

Although the French Impressionists were greatly influenced by the Dutch masters and lived during the Victorian period, they and the American Impressionists who followed them worked outside the tightly controlled, fussy forms then in fashion, often using flowers to experiment with composition and color harmonies. With few exceptions, the still lifes of the Impressionists have a carefree, relaxed style yet retain a strong sense of structure.

Of all cut flowers, carnations possess the longest vase life. Although sometimes considered commonplace, carnations offer the creative floral designer a wide range of colors with which to work. This dramatic arrangement capitalizes on the rainbow of colors found in the Nice farmers' market. Created by Carolyn for the dining room of the Renoir Museum, Cagnes-sur-Mer, the arrangement complements the beauty of the pottery vase made by Renoir's son Charles.

The Impressionists also lived during an era dubbed the Golden Age of Horticulture for the large number of new plants brought into cultivation at that time. The Impressionists' break from realism introduced new ways of looking at art, and the explosion in gardening introduced some sensational new motifs in the world of flowers. At the same time, the building of railways greatly enhanced mobility, making fresh flowers available in every season.

Floral still-life painting became extremely salable after Japan opened its borders to world trade and the Western world saw how beautifully the Japanese portrayed flowers in their art. By 1880, flowers were a favorite motif for many innovative artists. Although all were captivated by the color, form, and texture of flowers and foliage, each artist approached still-life painting in a different way. Many of Renoir's still lifes are delicate, highly detailed, intricate compositions, indicating that a great amount of thought and time went into the preparation of each arrangement before it was painted. Monet, on the other hand, liked more carefree arrangements, and Cezanne emphasized the flowers' structural qualities, giving more attention to the composition of stems and leaves than of blooms, while van Gogh expressed great passion in his choice of color. Collectively, their work makes an interesting study and provides us with ample inspiration for our own floral designs.

Inspired by Renoir's famous painting "Spring Bouquet," this arrangement in the garden at Cedaridge Farm uses a different palette of flowers to capture the spirit of Renoir's work. This exuberant arrangement uses old-fashioned flowers such as peonies, sweet William, and ox-eye daisies to echo the colors of the painting, though Renoir selected different flowers for his arrangement.

Claude Monet

Describing his own colorful style of painting, Monet once said his art was a record of "what I see, what I remember, and what I *feel*." It was the feeling contained in a scene captured on canvas that made Impressionism unique.

Monet's favorite subject was his garden, and he designed his dramatic plantings for the purpose of painting them, not caring about the ephemeral nature of some of the flowers. He was endlessly fascinated by the range and subtlety of the colors with which nature endowed plants, noting not only their brilliant shades but the sheen of their petals and foliage as well.

Although Monet painted still lifes only during inclement weather when he could not paint out in the garden, his ability to express feeling through his painting is evident in all his work. In his bold sweeps of color, dramatic color harmonies, careful selection of pleasing backgrounds, and obvious love of flowers, we see a fresh approach to floral art. For the painting "Two Vases of Chrysanthemums" (1888), for example, Monet seems to have picked an entire plant to use as an "instant bouquet," its tousled windblown flower heads looking as though they have just come in from the garden. His painting of an arrangement of sunflowers is simple in its informality, but he has carefully arranged the flowers so that their big, bold, golden heads are at distinctly different angles of view. He is always careful in his choice of container, generally preferring Oriental styles, and the vases are always in perfect balance with the arrangements.

Pierre-Auguste Renoir

Renoir also loved flowers, and his fascination with detail is reflected in his paintings of them. He painted a quick study every morning to refine his painting skills, saying that the soft colors and texture of rose petals helped him to capture the flesh tones of the women and children he loved to paint.

In his painting "Spring Bouquet" (1866), we see a very detailed use of flowers. The arrangement—thought to have been spotted by Renoir inside the salon of a wealthy art patron—was set on a stone balustrade outdoors so that it could be painted in the light. It is highly likely that Renoir rearranged the flowers before he painted the design. For example, a peony blossom has been taken out of the display and laid to the lower left of the vase to break up the severe lines of the balustrade. No doubt Renoir also discarded a few flowers that displeased him, leaving just the right balance of blues and pinks to satisfy his sense of color harmony and produce a predominantly blue and pink color combination (over time the pink pigments in the painting have faded somewhat and are now not so evident).

Also remarkable is Renoir's sophisticated use of white, which has been sprinkled liberally throughout the arrangement primarily as a filler and also to produce a glimmering sensation. The scattered white highlights the other flower colors without overwhelming them. Although the colors in the painting are soft, the flowers are presented in realistic detail, allowing us to identify the various plants (yellow wallflowers, yellow laburnum, blue lilacs, pink and white peonies, pink carnations, white bearded irises, white weigela, double white daisies, and a late-flowering white poet's daffodil).

Japanese in origin, the container's blue and white design not only echoes the blues and whites of the arrangement but appealed to the public's passion for Japanesque designs at the time. Blossoms of various sizes and shapes, an appealing color harmony, the natural placement of the flowers in the vase, and the magical use of glittering whites make the arrangement as well as the painting recognizable as a Renoir.

Van Gogh described the color combination of red and green as "passionate." In this inventive arrangement, the greens are mostly from leaves, while the vibrant reds include hot peppers, autumn-flowering roses, winterberry, and chrysanthemums.

Vincent van Gogh

Although van Gogh greatly admired the structural quality of certain floral arrangements (especially those that used ornamental grasses and wayside plants like thistles), his most significant contributions came from the vibrant color choices he made in his own compositions. Van Gogh stunned the world with masses of gorgeous golden sunflowers, pastel pink roses, and iridescent blue irises in sensational color combinations.

Van Gogh is a particularly good source of inspiration because, as a Postimpressionist, he not only learned a great deal from the paintings of Monet and Renoir, he was a prolific letter writer, explaining in minute detail the compositions of the arrangements he painted. He noted his reasons for choosing certain flowers to paint and also clarified his choice of background colors for them. (He sometimes rendered the same floral arrangement with different backgrounds to satisfy his passion for stimulating color couplings.)

Van Gogh's famous painting "Vase with Twelve Sunflowers" (1889) is but one example of his informal yet dramatic approach to still-life painting. The supreme simplicity of this painting's contents is largely responsible for the success of his approach. Using intense orange and yellow against a complementary pale blue background, van Gogh projected great energy and excitement, creating an impact on the visual senses that is quite possibly unsurpassed.

Significantly, van Gogh became fascinated with the sunflower as a subject and was passionate about the color yellow. He painted the same sunflower motif several times, using a fresh bouquet for each painting. Through this repetition he came closer and closer to what he considered to be the perfect balance of colors.

Cézanne's painting "The Blue Vase" served as a departure for this delicate arrangement. A strong vertical line and gently arching flowers create an open display, which is matched by the airy design of the wallpaper.

23

INSPIRATION

Paul Cézanne

Cézanne had a delicate hand with color, and in many of his floral still lifes, the hues all seem to be of the same intensity, successfully imitating the softness of works done with pastels. Cézanne's painting "The Blue Vase" (1883–1887) is one example of this phenomenon, and is composed primarily of two colors, pink and blue, a pairing much admired by the Impressionists. The addition of fruits on the table, the strong vertical of the vase, and an unexpected outstretched branch create stability and rhythm in the painting.

There is no question that the location of the vase is pivotal; we can see clearly the importance of strong structural lines, even though they are softened by the flower colors. Unrelated objects, in the form of fruit, add additional interesting shapes and colors. We can easily adapt and apply these principles, used so artfully by Cézanne, to our own flower arranging endeavors.

FOLLOWING IN THE FOOTSTEPS
OF THE FRENCH

Like the French Impressionists who inspired them, American Impressionists insisted on deviating from the conservative and often stiff designs that prevailed during the Victorian era. Their arrangements and paintings combined a natural, breezy quality with a passion for personal observation and a pleasing directness.

At about the same time van Gogh was painting, Childe Hassam (an American Impressionist trained in France) began painting flowers arranged by the American poet Celia Thaxter in her house on Appledore Island, off the coast of Maine. Through Hassam's paintings of her work, we can appreciate the beauty in her fresh, natural, and unaffected style of arranging flowers.

CONSTANCE SPRY AND BEYOND

In the mid-1930s, floral arranging took an entirely new direction in Europe and North America. It was Britain's Constance Spry who elevated floral arranging to a true art form, with guidelines and rules that were taught in schools founded specifically for floral design. For those involved in the floral art movement, words such as structure, style, form, balance, harmony, and rhythm became important concepts.

A self-taught gardener and plantsperson, Constance Spry began creating party decorations and special arrangements for friends in London. She met Sidney Bernstein, the owner of a chain of cinemas, and he commissioned her to create arrangements for both his home and the foyers of his cinemas. With the income she earned, Spry started her first store, called Flower Decorations, in a fashionable area of London. Bernstein also introduced Constance Spry to Norman Wilkinson, a noted stage designer, who invited her to create arrangements for the windows of Atkinson's, a leading perfumery on Old Bond Street and the most prestigious retail address in all of London. Illuminated at night, the stunning and unusual arrangements drew crowds of admirers, who marveled at her use of not only the usual cultivated flowers but also wildflowers, wayside plants, grasses, foliage, and exotic tropical plants, all elegantly ensconced in cornucopias, marble tazzas, and soapstone urns. Soon after her arrangements appeared, her own store became the trend-setting flower shop in London and her name—now synonymous with floral art—became famous throughout the world.

Noting that the results of World War II would bring drastic domestic changes and that multitudes of families would no longer be able to maintain household help, Spry set about teaching housewives how to decorate their own homes. To further this goal, she started a school designed to teach the full range of domestic arts, including flower arranging. In the process, Spry changed the way the Western world looks at an arrangement of flowers, just as the Impressionists changed the way the world appreciates great art.

Another development contributed to the breakthrough of flower arranging as an art in the West: in the 1940s, a firm, spongelike material called Oasis became available worldwide. A synthetic, easily pierced, solid substance, Oasis soaks up water quickly and holds stems rigid while allowing flowers to remain fresh. Almost overnight, the rarefied world of flower arranging became accessible to a war-weary population seeking color and cheer. In the 1950s and 1960s, flower arranging clubs became popular; they encouraged both the growing and

An explosion of flowers that combines both exotic blooms such as red anthuriums with familiar flowers like yellow Asiatic lilies, this large, formal arrangement is typical of the style of Constance Spry. The fan-shaped leaves of a palm provide balance, rhythm, and contrast within the design. Today, this type of stylized arrangement is most often seen in hotel and museum foyers, where the drama of intense colors can be fully appreciated.

arranging of flowers. Floral exhibitions and competitive shows were held at local, state, and national levels.

By the 1960s, the influence of Japanese styles of flower arranging began to make itself felt. The highly stylized art of ikebana—a form of flower arranging that had existed for centuries but was largely ignored and misunderstood in the West—suddenly gained favor in Western society, precipitating a popularity in line-style and other modernistic and futuristic types of floral designs.

With this proliferation of philosophies and styles, floral design has somehow become an enigma. In the chapters ahead, we'll examine the basic principles of good design and look more closely at color harmonies and the appropriateness of containers for various arrangements. Here, too, you'll find the assurance to approach the arranging of flowers with greater confidence and expanded creativity.

Favorite china patterns,

the subtle colors of table

linens, and the luminous

glazes of pottery pieces

can all provide wonder-

ful inspirations for

arrangements. Here,

blush pink double

'Angelique' tulips echo

the colors of delicate

porcelain flowers that

adorn a Victorian-style

vase.

DRAWING INSPIRATION FROM LIFE

With a genuine gratitude in our hearts for the inspirations of past artists and arrangers, we turn to our immediate surroundings for fresh revelations. At our home, Cedaridge Farm, we like to use an eclectic and somewhat haphazard collection of articles from the past in our decor. Old Amish quilts hang on walls and are draped across every bed. Collections of faded floral pillows from the 1920s and 1930s adorn every chair and couch, not merely for the sake of appearances but with the intention that they be used. (Sometimes, in early evening, these treasures are carried outside and piled in the hammock that hangs between two old sugar maple trees, making the perfect berth for a before-dinner nap.) Lace curtains, lending the ambience of a Victorian parlor, veil the windows of our house, and dried flowers hang from ceiling beams and decorate the mantels above stone fireplaces. Mismatched wicker chairs are scattered through the house and spill out onto the lawn. Old porch rockers line a balcony on which friends and family can relax and enjoy an elevated view of the garden vistas.

Carpets, wall coverings, paintings, and collectibles—such as porcelain dolls, Ohio pottery, and antique linens—reflect our personal tastes and often dictate the way we use flowers to decorate our rooms. Just as the living spaces reflect our relaxed lifestyle, our floral arrangements echo the same love of old-fashioned color and Impressionist motifs.

The wallpaper in a room can be a wonderful source of inspiration for floral designs, and at Cedaridge Farm, we have deliberately chosen papers that have floral motifs with a view to enhancing our flower arrangements. The master bedroom features a Victorian-style rose pattern in reds and strong rosy pinks; an adjacent bathroom is bedecked with a sweet pea motif in pastel colors. These rooms come alive when flower arrangements complement the floral wallpaper motifs, especially when the colors in the wallpaper are echoed in the arrangement.

Having looked at the past and seen the development of flower arranging styles—from simple posies to lavish mixed displays—and at the world around us for added inspiration, we can now focus on the modern concepts of design and seek new ways of expression for our ideas.

In the sunroom at Cedaridge Farm an old rocking chair, faded pillows, and a wicker plant stand contribute to the old farmhouse atmosphere. Buckets and baskets overflowing with freshly cut tulips in shades of pale to deep pink are clustered casually, creating a springtime display that is in perfect harmony with its surroundings.

CHAPTER 2

Essentials of Design

"What I am sure of is that to make a picture…it is not enough to have a certain cleverness. It is looking at things for a long time that ripens you and gives you a deeper understanding."

Vincent van Gogh

in a letter to his brother Theo

Dahlias and chrysanthemums, massed here in a stunning monochromatic design, bloom in autumn in shades of orange and yellow. These russet and golden tones echo the fall colors seen through the window.

M ost forms of design or creative expression require an outline or map to ensure that the final work lives up to the promise of the initial concept. The same holds true in arranging flowers, where we must take into consideration four essential points: style, color, structure, and texture. In planning for these basic elements of design, we create a blueprint that guarantees a memorable floral arrangement.

Bright-colored gladiolus and black-eyed Susans are arranged in a fan-shaped mass-style design.

STYLE

Style is the "nameplate" for the arrangement; it defines our vision for the design and provides a useful set of terms for discussing its elements. An arrangement is most often recognizable as formal or informal, or traditional or contemporary; these labels are attached based largely on a design's shape or outline. Additional terms help us express our ideas and aid us in our choice of style as we begin an arrangement. Terms such as front-facing, triangular, horizontal, vertical, and all-around (to be viewed from any direction) describe an outline that becomes the final shape of an arrangement. Although these terms are important, they refer to one-dimensional aspects of the arrangement. To create a multidimensional look, we must go further, and describe mass, line, line-mass, and miscellaneous styles.

Mass Style

The mass style is full, robust, and colorful, reminiscent of the designs of the past often tagged as European style. Mass style is discussed in terms such as rounded or domed, fan-shaped, triangular, cylindrical, or cone-shaped. Most often, the mass style is expressed in all-around designs created on a vertical axis with equidistant horizontal lines defining the outer edges. This outline is filled in, making the entire arrangement full of blossoms. Because it is most often intended to be viewed from any side, there is little need for a central focal point. Instead of attempting to create a focal point in a mass-style arrangement, rely on a smooth transition between the elements to make a pleasing design, and allow the varying colors and sizes of blooms to create interest throughout the arrangement.

The very formal mass style often seen at special events such as weddings, although beautiful, may seem overstudied in relaxed settings. Slight deviations from the design's shape, along with an effort to position the flowers in a natural way, can lend a more usual air to a mass-style arrangement. At Cedaridge Farm we often use mass styles for our arrangements, as their robust beauty is in perfect harmony with many of the flowers we enjoy. With carefully orchestrated flower colors and a variety of blossom shapes and sizes, we strive for a strong feeling of movement throughout the design and often flirt with an unrelated or discordant color, a device that the artist Paul Gauguin used very effectively in many of his paintings.

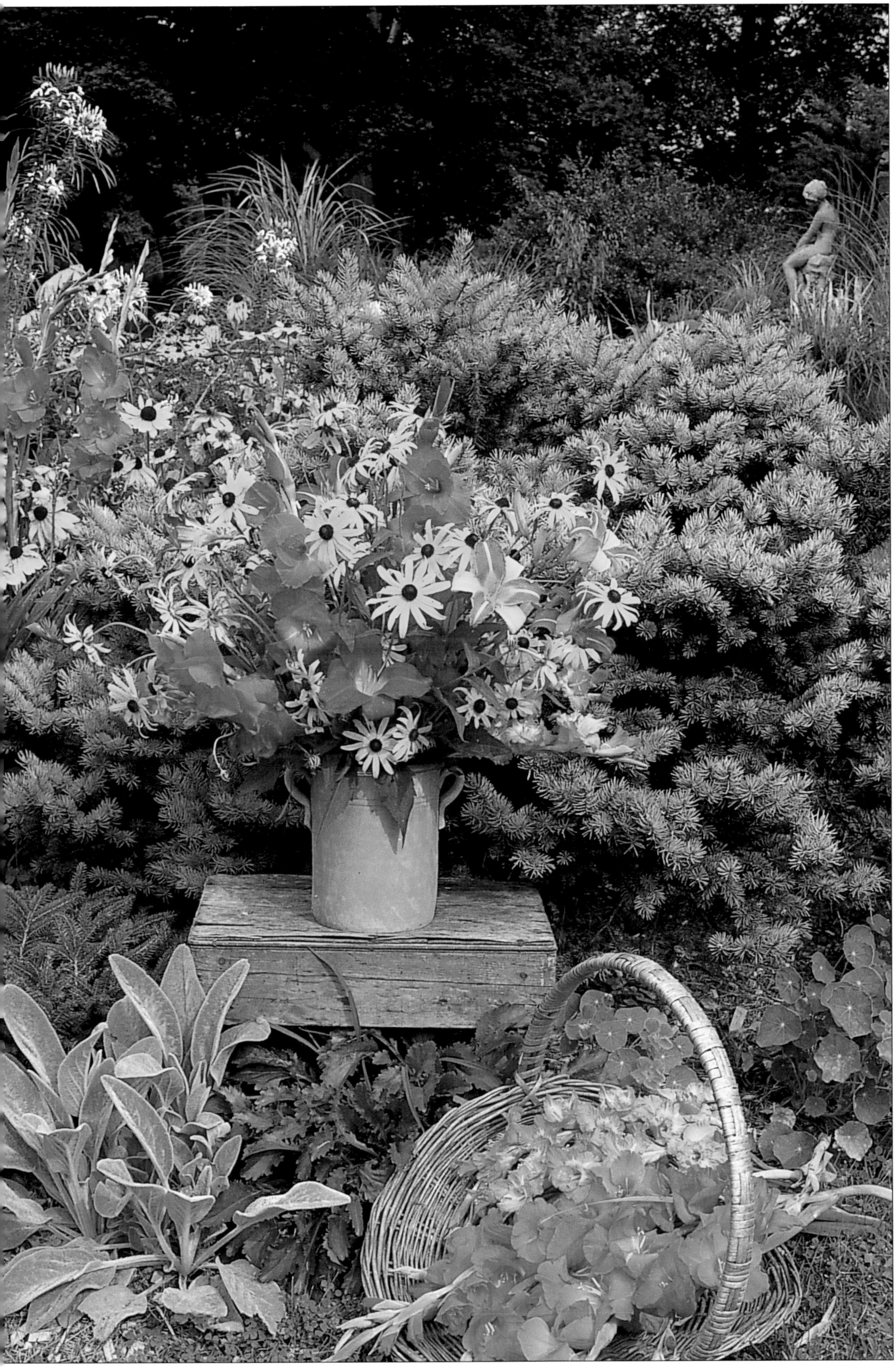

Line Style

In contrast to mass style, arrangements executed in line style are tall and sparse. This style is reflective of Oriental designs, for which basic rules were established more than a thousand years ago. Blooms such as chrysanthemums and peonies and flowering tree branches like plum and apricot were held in high regard—the garden flowers were admired for their flamboyance, the branches for their strong sculptural lines. The Japanese style of floral display dates back to the sixteenth century and is thought to have been taken to Japan from China by missionary Buddhist priests. To this day, Japanese floral design is the most studied of all floral techniques; it follows rigid rules governing the types of plants, their precise use, and the container in which they are presented. Simple in line, the arrangements follow a basic formula that incorporates three elements: heaven (tallest), man (middle), and earth (lowest). The art of Japanese flower arranging, most widely called ikebana, involves more than simply grouping flowers—it is a spiritual expression, full of symbolism, and travels far beyond a mere afternoon activity.

The French Impressionist painters were captivated by Japanese art and its portrayal of flower arrangements. Monet and van Gogh both owned large collections of Japanese wood block prints, and both admired the Japanese aesthetic, especially that of the Japanese artisan.

Our Western line design was greatly influenced by these Eastern expressions, which began to be familiar to Europeans and Americans, particularly in the years after World War II, though they did not gain widespread popularity in North America until the 1950s. Using only a few flowers or leaves to create the design, a line arrangement depends on the use of space between the elements to complete the design. Tall, sinuous, gnarled branches, interesting seedpods, curly willow, tall flower stems with single flower heads, and spiky flowers like veronica and larkspur all create strong vertical lines. Terms used to identify line style are vertical, free-style, abstract, modern, and futuristic.

Line arrangements can appear very stiff and impersonal, though they need not be so. A good line arrangement—in which careful attention has been given to the plants used and their disposition in the design—will have a relaxed elegance. Certain varieties of flowers and grasses are dramatic when arranged in the line style—calla lilies, with their flared, chalicelike flowers; birds-of-paradise, with their angular flower form; and pampas grass, with its silky, silvery plumes are all elegant candidates. Tulips—with their bowl-shaped flowers and long, erect stems—present interesting possibilities because a tulip continues to grow once it is severed from its bulb. This stretching nature of the tulip is capitalized on in terms of design, and its curving stem creates a beautiful, arching, natural line. Tall, narrow containers also emphasize vertical line, even though the floral contents may be soft.

Line-Mass Style

Not surprisingly, line-mass style results from a combination of line style and mass style. This is the style of design preferred in most of the French Impressionists' still lifes and is the favored one here at Cedaridge Farm for the relaxed designs that evoke a mellow country mood. Borrowing elements from both line and mass disciplines, the line-mass style can express many moods. The focal point may be on one central flower, a movement of flowers throughout the design, or an explosive grouping with a wide circle of rhythm. In general, the mass, or greatest density, is near the lower central axis, that which is closest to the container. The line component is introduced by nonconforming elements such as tall single flowers, flower buds, or grasses or twigs that reach beyond the mass; these features create a rhythm and direct the eye from the edges of the arrangement back to the central focal point.

This vertical line-mass arrangement is composed of what we affectionately call "mere garden gatherings"—flowers are collected for individual blossom beauty as we walk through the garden, without any intent to create a particular arrangement. The outcome is always amazing. This collection of giant allium, foxgloves, peonies, the old English rose 'Gertrude Jekyll,' an iris, and a few stems of painted daisy is reminiscent of many of Vincent van Gogh's still-life floral paintings.

A mass of mixed lark-spur, variously colored cornflowers, and chartreuse lady's mantle compose this all-around symmetrical arrangement. Because the cornflowers and larkspur are of similar shades, the contrasting flower shapes are critical in providing visual interest in this design.

SYMMETRICAL AND ASYMMETRICAL DESIGNS

The above three styles—mass, line, and line-mass—are further divided into two distinct classifications: symmetrical and asymmetrical. Both depend on balance to make a successful flower arrangement.

Symmetrical Designs

Symmetrical designs are dependent upon the repetition of flowers and equal visual weight on both sides of the arrangement. The most familiar symmetrical designs are mass arrangements in the shape of a dome, fan, or triangle, all of which are usually seen in formal displays, most often at special events such as weddings.

Fortunately, our tastes are broadening, and symmetrical designs are becoming more popular for all sorts of uses. A beautiful arrangement of flowers can be in a symmetrical form without appearing rigid. Symmetrically balanced arrangements can be achieved by using flower forms or colors that are varied but carry equal visual weight. For example, a few brilliant red and red-orange garden lilies can be visually balanced by a group of yellow gloriosa daisies. The mass of yellow and the combination of red and red-orange offset each other handsomely.

Asymmetrical Designs

Asymmetrical line designs, on the other hand, are highly dependent on the line of the arrangement being different on either side of the center. This can be achieved by using different colors

Dried flowers adorn this Christmas tree, reminiscent of Byzantine-influenced cone-shaped symmetrical arrangements. The wreath, which we commonly associate with Christmas, is one of the most ancient forms of flower arranging.

and textures on the left and right sides or simply by varying the placement of the same types of flowers used on both sides. Asymmetrical style can be intensely dramatic, highly formal, or completely informal, depending on the flowers used and the character of the container.

MISCELLANEOUS STYLES

There are several styles of flower arranging that do not fit firmly within our basic classifications of mass, line, and line-mass styles. These arrangements do not radiate from one point, that is, they do not issue forth from the top of a single container.

Wreaths, swags, and garlands, for example, do not conform to any of the above principles, yet these sorts of arrangements are the oldest form of floral design. These circles and ropes of flowers are held together by the use of wire, floral foam, or glue, and both fresh and dried flowers are commonly used. Wreaths and garlands are especially popular for holidays and special events, and can be used to add freshness and a sense of the outdoors to an interior decor. Topiaries, a twentieth-century addition to the art of floral design, are constructed by placing flowers around a three-dimensional form such as a sphere or cone.

Another miscellaneous type of arrangement consists of grouping similar arrangements or potted blooms to create a theme. Often, candles are added, giving height and drama to a table centerpiece.

A third group of miscellaneous arrangements includes landscape arrangements. Usually placed on a piece of wood or board, these arrangements are intended to represent a place, like an island paradise or the corner of a cottage garden.

The importance of creative color choice and thoughtful placement of blossoms is evident in this massed arrangement composed of flowers in analogous colors, including pink obedient plant; scarlet, rose, and pink gladiolus; and rosy-pink cornflowers. Pale yellow walls add further depth and excitement to this subtle but sensational color harmony.

COLOR

Color, the most important visual component of an arrangement, is essential to any design. Good use of color aids the movement of the eye through a design by mixing tints and tones of a particular color and also by making use of analogous colors (those adjacent to each other on the color wheel). Color also creates mood—white is romantic, black is sinister, red is hot, blue is cool— and helps identify a seasonal aspect—russet colors indicate autumn, pale pink has strong springtime connotations.

Color also requires a basic understanding of the color wheel. In the chapter on color, we will look more closely at scientific color theory and how it helps us in arranging flowers more successfully.

STRUCTURE

Structure is the basic shape of the design and applies to both formal and informal arrangements. If we desire a starburst effect, then we must consider stiff, strong, spiky flowers like gladiolus and delphiniums; if we want a cascading effect, then the weeping stems of bleeding heart and trailing ivy are most effective. Cézanne considered structure the most important element in an arrangement, and created definite horizontal and vertical lines throughout his still-life paintings. Renoir emphasized structure in a softer way, grouping heavy-headed peonies in a gently sweeping design or letting them tumble out of a vase. Van Gogh enjoyed strong lines that crossed in angles or shot off into space, often creating contorted shapes.

TEXTURE

Texture in flower arrangements is more visual than tactile. It is impossible to create a floral arrangement that does not contain texture, for all plants have their own specific textural qualities. The petals of many flowers—poppies and cosmos, for example—are translucent with a satiny sheen. Tulips and gladiolus have a slick, waxy look, while bee balm and sea urchin cacti look rather prickly. Other plants, such as baby's breath and Russian sage, are light and airy. These traits combine to impart a quality of texture to any flower arrangement.

Choosing leaves to complement the flowers in the arrangement is important to the design's texture. Like flower petals, leaves can be soft and matte (like those of lady's mantle), shiny (like holly leaves), leathery (like the leaves of the southern magnolia), prickly (like Scotch thistles), or blistered (like many hostas' leaves). Leaves can also have edges that are sharp or serrated and surfaces that are soft, smooth, ribbed, dull, or woolly.

Twigs, branches, and vines are also important considerations for texture. Many trees and shrubs, such as willow, paper birch, and paperbark maple, have smooth, scaly, or peeling bark that can make an interesting addition to a creative arrangement. Elements such as rose hips, pinecones, or clusters of grapes also contribute interesting textural qualities.

The essentials of design become second nature with experimentation and practice, but the learning process is never complete, for each new arrangement offers fresh discoveries.

Texture is the raison d'être for this dramatic arrangement: shards of brown tree bark, contorted willow branches, and matte green leaves combine with glossy red anthuriums to create exciting contrasts.

Elements of a Successful

Arrangement

"I want to get my drawings more spontaneous.

I'm trying now to exaggerate the essential,

and…to leave the obvious vague."

Vincent van Gogh

in a letter to his brother Theo

Bunching smaller flowers, such as the pink carnations in this arrangement,
produces a greater mass of color and allows more specific definition
of flowers that would otherwise be insignificant in a composition.

All the elements of a successful floral composition are represented in this vibrant summer arrangement: each flower is easily identified; the size and placement of each element creates harmony; the use of flowers with varying visual weights establishes good proportion; and foliage contrasts give the design added distinction.

hen you become more familiar with the art of flower arranging, you will be able to recognize certain signatures or styles of design associated with particular people or places. For example, the exuberant style of Constance Spry is easily identified; at the other extreme is the highly simplistic but dramatic style of van Gogh, which is perhaps even more familiar. We have a friend in New Zealand, Olive Dunn, whose creative designs are instantly recognizable because she uses only fresh flowers from her garden, has impeccable taste in color, and sites her floral creations in her charming house filled with Victoriana, which sets off her designs.

There is no reason why anyone cannot become well known (locally or internationally) for a distinctive and original style of flower arranging. In addition to the choice of flowers, the following elements of design are responsible for successful, stimulating arrangements: clarity, harmony, and proportion.

CLARITY

A good design must have clarity, that is, a clear focus or message. In arranging flowers, each flower or textured leaf chosen by the arranger must be important to the overall design. Although each flower is part of the larger arrangement, its individuality must shine through. Every flower has a specific place within the design, and based upon its color, shape, or form, it helps create a coherent composition.

Grouping small flowers together (called "bunching") to form a mass of color is the best way to display the distinctive form of a particular flower family, such as coreopsis, star zinnias, or miniature roses. Placing flowers on different planes—not directly on top of or directly next to each other—can make arrangements look less rigid while retaining clarity. Nor do all flowers have to face forward; by placing flowers at natural angles and by using the backs of flowers, we can create serene and charming designs.

Clarity is enhanced when like colors or similar tones are placed together, making a smooth transition from one strong color to another, just as artists mix paints to create shadowy color between two bold hues. In arranging flowers, we can use two closely related colors to create this painterly effect, for example, placing soft blue ageratum next to violet blue salvia before situating them beside orange or yellow dahlias. By arranging the colors in this manner, we avoid a choppy composition full of colors vying for attention.

HARMONY

In a musical composition, each note flows smoothly into the next and a sour note is quickly recognized; in a flower arrangement, clashing colors and shapes are equally distressing. We

Proportion in an arrangement is directly related to the balance of the contents. Beautiful spring flowers, each compatible with the others and all in proper scale, fill this delicate Mother's Day basket. Allowing a few sprigs of white spirea to extend beyond the boundaries of the design gives a fresh airy feeling to the composition.

must train our eyes to see these clashing "sounds" in a design. In addition to conflicting shapes and colors, arrangements that are too large or too small for the setting or simply out of character for their location or container are hallmarks of poor design.

Pleasing harmony within a design includes proper balance and a sense of unity. Unity is the impression of the arrangement as a coherent whole; it is the combination of all the parts in a satisfying solidarity. If the parts clash or jostle for attention within the design, the arrangement will lack unity and will be troubling to the viewer. We can see this in arrangements that have too much space between flowers or in those where flowers are crammed too tightly into the container. Harmony within an arrangement is important if the design is to win praise. Dissonance in color, shape, or content can be beautiful but the discordant elements must be chosen with purpose and must be harmonious within the context of the total composition. The Postimpressionist painter Gauguin is a particularly good artist to study for touches of discord in harmonious color—he often adds a splash of red in a cool color harmony of blue, mauve, and purple or a dab of bright yellow in a harmony of pink and blues.

Good color harmony is essential when matching an arrangement to a particular location. Generally, the location not only dictates the style of the design—a low centerpiece for a dining table, a tall accent piece for a foyer—but also the colors that will be used. If the foyer is dark, an arrangement full of dark tones would most likely be a poor choice, because the lack of light would render any harmony within the arrangement invisible.

PROPORTION

Proportion is an aspect of harmony essential to good design. All other elements can be properly in place, but if the design is poorly proportioned, it will be jarring. Flowers too large for their container or groupings of flowers that are incompatible—like orchids and daisies—will doom an arrangement from the start. The age-old rule for checking proportion is still a good way to ensure that your design will have pleasant dimensions: for a tall container, the arrange-

ment's total height may be 1½ times the height of the container; for a short container, the height may reach 1½ times the width of the container. Although this is a basic guideline, it can produce a very rudimentary design if followed too rigidly. A top-heavy arrangement made of large, weighty flowers like dahlias placed in a slender vase will not just appear to be falling over, it probably will. By comparison, a big, heavy container should be filled with blossoms that can balance the mass of the urn.

Good proportion is directly related to balance, which can be explored in either symmetrical or asymmetrical terms. In symmetrical designs such as a cone- or fan-shape, the sides mirror each other; in asymmetrical arrangements, opposite sides are purposefully different from each other. These designs are where balance and proportion meet. A well-balanced asymmetrical design is often the most difficult to arrange successfully, but we find it to be the most satisfying because of its irregular shape and the energetic movement within the design. The rhythm of an asymmetrical arrangement is created by balance and counterbalance as each flower is added to the container. Simply choosing a branch with great shape and form can be the beginning of an exciting arrangement, and you need only add a few flowers or grasses to complete a beautiful, natural-looking display.

Determining the focal point of a design is important to its overall proportion. A focal point does not have to be obvious, and in fact, the more subtle it is, the more fascinating the arrangement becomes. These accents add excitement to a design and must be carefully placed to create the most dramatic effect. Something as simple as a light-colored flower placed at an unusual angle can be the focal point. Van Gogh was an expert at placing just the right accents in his still-life paintings. Most often he used the implication of light to create a focal point, making it appear as though a beam of light was cast upon the chosen flowers.

The joy of working with arrangements is in making them distinctive. The ultimate thrill comes when we develop a style that is a reflection of our own sensibilities. A unique personal style evolves not only through individual preferences in design but also in the selection of flowers and the way we choose to present them.

All of the elements in an arrangement must work together in harmonious balance. Likewise, a design must fit comfortably in the location where it is to be viewed. Through the balance of contents, color choice, texture, and accents, an arrangement achieves unity of design. The autumnal hues of this fan-shaped chrysanthemum and goldenrod design make an attractive Thanksgiving decoration on the small shelf of an antique cabinet.

43

ELEMENTS
OF A
SUCCESSFUL
ARRANGEMENT

CHAPTER 4

Color

"What color is to a picture,

enthusiasm is in life."

Vincent van Gogh

in a letter to his brother Theo

Considered a "cool" color harmony, this grouping of pink and mauve summer flowers uses 'Flamingo Feather' celosias, 'Fairy' roses, 'Seashells' cosmos, and ivy-leaf geraniums. The entire grouping seems to recede, creating a quiet look that conveys a feeling of fragility.

fter exploring sources of inspiration and studying the various elements of design, we are ready to look more closely at what we believe to be the most important part of any flower arrangement—color.

There are several ways to "look" at color. One method is to expose the colors in sunlight by holding a crystal up to the light: what we see is prismatic color, the seven colors of the rainbow—red, orange, yellow, green, blue, indigo, and violet. The world of plants, however, is composed of many more subtle variations in color, some of them extremely difficult to classify because all colors are affected by the dynamics of light. Bright light, for instance, can make certain blue flowers appear purple, and dim light can make blue seem to disappear entirely.

The brilliant use of harmonious colors—possible because of the artists' understanding of scientific color theory—helps make Impressionism the most admired art form in the world. More than any other aspect of flower arranging, color can make your arrangements both beautiful and unique.

Unveiling the Mysteries of the Color Wheel

It was not until the early 1800s that the scientific world explored the wonders of color more closely, revealing the relationships between colors. Michel-Eugène Chevreul, director of dye quality control at the Gobelins tapestry workshop in France, published the first scientific analysis of color, producing what we now refer to as the color wheel—an arrangement of colors that shows how they are related and how the source of all color is three primary colors. He identified red, yellow, and blue as primary colors, each having equal weight. By mixing each of these three colors with one of the others, in equal proportions, three additional colors could be created—orange (red with yellow), green (yellow with blue), and violet (blue with red). He called these mixes secondary colors, and together with the primary colors they comprise a complete circle of six major colors (see Appendix on page 124).

Chevreul identified as complementary colors those that do not share the same pigment, or, in other words, colors that are across the color wheel from each other—such as red and green, blue and orange, yellow and violet. These, he advised, made the strongest, most pleasing, and most dramatic combinations. On the other hand, those colors that share a hue in their makeup (these are adjacent on the color wheel) are the most harmonious and pleasing to the eye—such as yellow with green or orange, blue with green or violet, and red with violet or orange.

Though scientific color theory is useful in creating pleasing color harmonies, the Impressionist painters stressed as well the value of seeking the best color combinations in nature. Here, the colors of a summer sunset—reds, oranges, and yellows—create a vibrant display.

46
COLOR

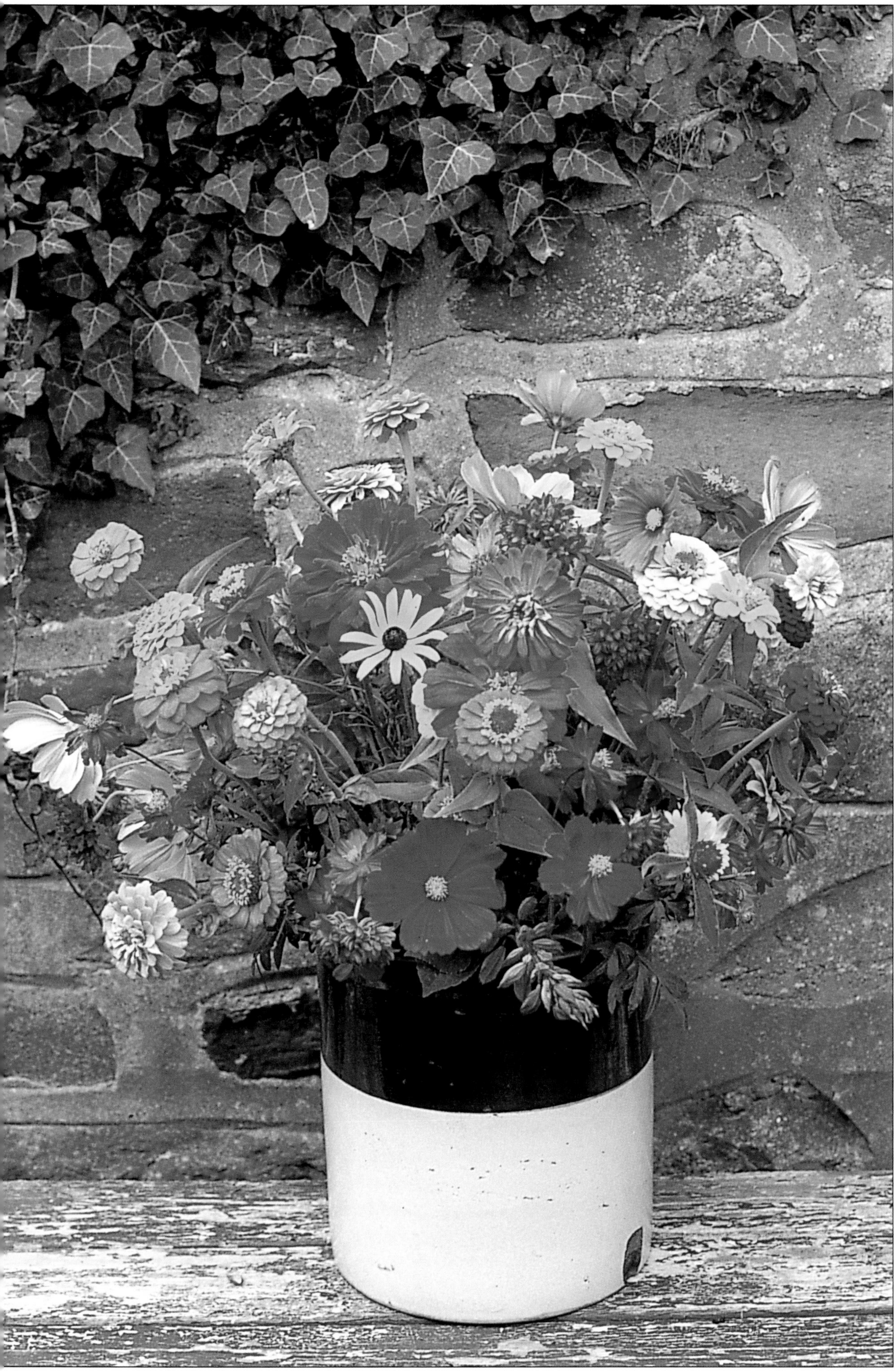

Monochromatic harmonies can be very successful when one plant variety is used. Pictured here are sweet Williams in many variations of red, including an array of pinks. The gradations of color and the slightly irregular mound shape of the composition give this monochromatic design visual interest.

In between all the major colors of the color wheel, which are called hues, are more subtle gradations of color. These are referred to as shades, which are created by the addition of black; tints, which are created by the addition of white; and tones, which are created by the addition of gray. Combining the various hues, shades, tints, and tones in pleasing ways is referred to as creating color harmonies.

A monochromatic harmony consists of tints, tones, and shades of the same hue—for example, red (hue), pink (tint), scarlet red (tone), and ruby red (shade). In general, monochromatic arrangements are the easiest to assemble, but care must be exercised to avoid making the arrangement look boring. Refrain from arranging the flowers and leaves in a regimented way, and use blooms in varying stages of maturity—for example, an arrangement of pink peonies may include singles, doubles, and buds, with some of the flowers on short stems and others on long stems.

Analogous color harmonies make use of colors adjacent to each other on the color wheel, such as violet, red-violet, and blue-violet or yellow, yellow-green, and yellow-orange. Analogous color arrangements are probably the most common, and they are often the most successful in expressing a mood. Red, orange, and yellow, for example, are the colors of the sunset, and together they express great energy and warmth.

Complementary harmonies consist of colors opposite each other on the color wheel, such as red and green, orange and blue, or yellow and violet. These are the color combinations most often seen in Impressionist paintings. Van Gogh, in explaining the laws of colors to his sister, expressed the opinion that complementary colors were wedded like man and woman. These colors are safe pairings, often used for large arrangements intended to grace foyers and dining rooms.

Three colors equidistant on the color wheel—such as red, yellow, and blue, or orange, green, and violet—make up a triadic harmony. The difficulty with this type of color combination is that all three colors are equally strong. To create a pleasing triadic harmony, make use of varying tints, tones, and shades of the three colors. By choosing one hue to take a major role and by supporting this color selection with tints, tones, and shades of the remaining two colors in the triad, you'll get a truly striking result. It's also critical to vary the type of blossoms in a triadic color harmony: all one flower type or shape (all spiky blooms, for instance) is repetitious in a displeasing way.

Polychromatic harmonies employ numerous colors, like the rainbow, in a pleasant arrangement that avoids a hodgepodge effect. Garden flowers lend themselves nicely to polychromatic arrangements, where hybridized flowers, twigs, and wildflowers can be grouped together successfully. Good polychromatic color harmonies rely upon the use of texture and a wide variety of blossom types to create a dramatic display. The colors used are subordinate to the style and exuberance of the blossoms, which carry the design. Therefore, clarity and harmony are extremely important to the success of polychromatic designs and ensure that the entire arrangement makes a strong statement. The asymmetrical line-mass style of arranging is very useful in this multicolored style of display—it allows the arrangement to appear airy and unstructured. Paintings of the Dutch masters are good studies for this type of color harmony.

A solid understanding of these color harmonies is useful when arranging flowers. Flowers are not like paint: we cannot "mix" a color. Therefore, it is important to understand what happens when colors are situated next to each other, and we must learn how much or how little of each color is appropriate, as well as the way the size and shape of a flower affect its dynamics in an arrangement.

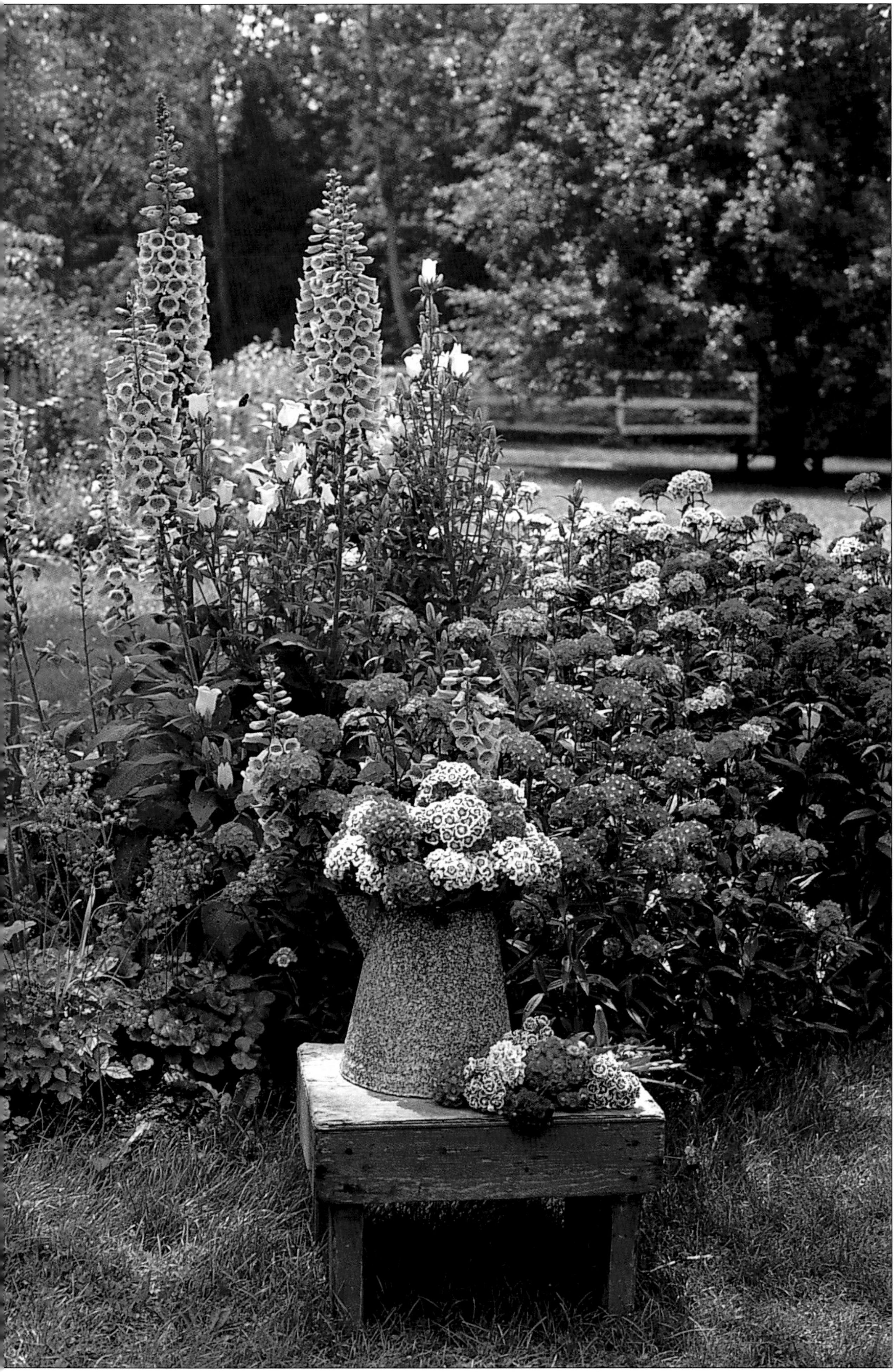

Many flowers, such as these cosmos, are especially beautiful when positioned so that light can pass through the translucent petals. The white and pink blossoms take on a delicate glow when sunlight filters through the window, illluminating this cheerful arrangement composed of analogous hues.

Light

The intensity of light plays a role in the way colors appear. Bright, diffuse sunlight will enliven colors; the less light there is, the darker a color appears. Total darkness kills all color, with dark colors—like blue and violet—disappearing first. At the other extreme, the bright, glaring sunlight of a cloudless day can make pastel colors seem bleached or washed out. Pastel colors come alive in moonlight and are good for use in arrangements that will be placed on a deck in summer. Whites, of course, show up well in moonlight, but also consider lemon yellows and pale pinks.

Artificial light can change the appearance of certain flower colors significantly. If the light source is a tungsten bulb, cool colors will be duller, and warm colors will appear brighter. The light from fluorescent tubes produces the opposite effect: cool colors are brightened and warm colors are dulled. Candlelight dims cool colors and adds yellow tones to warm colors.

Translucence is another important factor in choosing colors and flower types. Although arrangements should not be placed in strong direct sunlight, which can wilt flowers, window ledges are perfect for displaying flowers. By choosing flowers with petals that glow when backlit—such as cosmos and lilies—you can create a dreamy effect reminiscent of a Chinese lantern.

Colors have personalities, the most common categories being hot or cool. Red is a hot color that is often described as "passionate." It appears to advance and dominate, while yellow—also a hot color—is bright and uplifting. Indeed, we often describe yellow as "cheerful." Blue, violet, and mauve tend to be cool colors; they are soft and receding. Pink is the most common color in all the flower kingdom, and in its lighter forms it tends to be tranquil. Black, the least common flower color, is sinister when used in excess but is often marvelous in contrast with white and orange. Gray and green are considered cool colors, but they are also good mixers and are often used as "knitting" colors. White and silver can add lightness and sparkle to arrangements. By looking at the shades and tints of a color, we can gain a better understanding of how diverse a color can be.

Black

At Cedaridge Farm, during research for a book on Impressionist flower gardens, we discovered a color combination we had never before seen used with flowers—the combination of black and white! The idea of using black and white flowers in an arrangement came to us from letters written by van Gogh naming his favorite color contrasts and also from an analysis of Monet's famous painting "Magpie"—a black and white motif now displayed in the

Pairings of black and white flowers, inspired by the paintings of Monet and van Gogh, have become a favorite color harmony at Cedaridge Farm. Tall spiky hollyhocks in black and porcelain white create the dramatic structure of this arrangement. The bold hollyhocks are complemented by smaller white flowers such as irises, feverfew, garden phlox, astilbe, and garden roses.

51

COLOR

Snowballs of phlox placed freely throughout the arrangement lend this display an easy, relaxed appearance. The white phlox echoes the white in the tablecloth motif, thereby bringing the unusual flower selection—which also includes hollyhocks and caladium leaves—for this basket centerpiece into focus.

Orsay Museum in Paris. Van Gogh painted many black and white floral arrangements (using deep maroon to represent black). Monet's "Magpie" shows a black and white bird sitting on a wattle fence in a snow-covered garden.

Although there are very few flowers in nature that can be called black, the color black can be added to an arrangement by incorporating flowers with black or near-black centers, such as black-eyed Susans, some sunflowers, and many African daisies. Also, there are maroon flowers that can substitute for black to achieve a similar stunning contrast. These include "black" pansies like 'Molly Sanderson' and the dark maroon forms of hollyhocks, scabiosa, nasturtiums, and peonies, which are often referred to as black. Of all the "black" flowers available to the flower arranger, none is more beautiful in our minds than the black hollyhock. Its spire-like flower stems are studded with saucer-shaped blooms that combine well with many white cut flowers, especially phlox, foxgloves, and hostas.

There are also black fruits, such as black raspberries, blackberries, black figs, and black gooseberries, which can help make an arrangement truly sensational.

White

An entire book could be written about the use of white in flower arrangements. The most common mistake when arranging with white flowers is to bunch them too tightly; this results in visual "holes" in the arrangement. Chevreul pointed out that white tends to brighten the colors adjacent to it. For example, a solid blue sky can appear dark, but with a few fluffy white clouds, the blue suddenly brightens. White goes well not only with blue but with many other colors. It is especially pleasing when used with pink, or with blue and pink in combination, for example, in a wedding bouquet.

The glitter, glimmer, and shimmer characteristic of white captivated the Impressionists. Monet capitalized on the sparkling sensation in his garden by planting airy white flowers like baby's breath and dame's rocket liberally throughout the garden. He also carried this impression of glitter high into the sky by training airy vines of white clematis along arbors and trellises. White baby's breath and sweet autumn clematis will have the same effect in flower arrangements. The airy sprays of baby's breath make good filler material to brighten solid colors, but because baby's breath tends to be overused in floral arrangements, we prefer to use less-familiar substitutes like chamomile and Queen Anne's lace. Similarly, the clematis vine can be intertwined with other flowers—like threads of wool in a coat—to brighten arrangements.

Be aware that white also has the ability to reflect adjacent colors, just as a sunset will be reflected in the bark of a white birch, giving the white bark an apricot or pink tinge.

Silver

Silver is very close to white and can be used in much the same way as white, even appearing natural in a monochromatic white arrangement. Although we know of few plants with silver flowers (some forms of sea holly have silvery flower bracts), we know of many with silvery leaves (such as artemisia and lamb's ears). Some flower arrangers, particularly those in Europe, describe these leaves as gray, but we prefer the more commonly used appellation of silver because it is actually more descriptive of their effect. Monet found that silvery leaves like dianthus and lamb's ears were good in combination with red and pink, and silver is also stunning with blue. In fact, it is hard to go wrong with silver. Think of it as a good alternative—as well as a good complement—to green.

The patterns, textures, and colors of leaves create a welcoming montage on the front porch at Cedaridge Farm. No matter what the season, the front porch always features a striking arrangement.

Green

In flower arranging, green is a very important color because it is the color against which most flowers must contrast. It is the color of grass, evergreens, and the forest. Green is made up of blue and yellow, and some greens tend more toward one of the component hues than the other—these are generally known as yellow-greens or blue-greens. There are also light greens like apple green, midgreens like mint green, and dark greens like forest green. The darker greens are almost impossible to find in the petal colors of flowers but are available in some fruits, such as avocado, and of course in many kinds of foliage. There are few combinations more certain to stun an audience than the uncommon light greens of certain flowers or fruits mixed with the darker greens of leaves. Some good examples of green flowers are bells of Ireland, 'Green Envy' zinnias, the miniature rose 'Green Ice', 'St. Patrick's' gladiolus, and 'Really Green' nicotiana. Many plants outside the traditional cutting garden make dramatic green accents, such as dill, asparagus ferns, and hops. Vegetables and fruits such as green tomatoes, pea pods, and 'Granny Smith' apples are also good for adding interest and variety to an arrangement.

Do not overlook flowers that have green eyes, like old-fashioned 'Madame Hardy' damask roses or 'Cheerful White' stocks. Make use of the green in unopened flowers, such as the tips of gladiolus or chincherinchee, which can add strong lines and texture to an arrangement. Leaves, of course, also play an important role in floral arrangements, their abundant green contrasting well with all colors. Hosta leaves offer a wide variety of shades, from blues to citron yellows, while feathery ferns and smooth-leafed pachysandra contribute intriguing texture.

Yellow

Van Gogh loved the color yellow—which he found to be much more intense in the light of southern France than in his homeland of Holland—and he used it liberally and exuberantly. Yellow is a primary color that has green to one side of it on the color wheel and orange to the other; its range of tints, tones, and shades include cream, gold, and mustard. Because it is so widely represented in the floral world, yellow is an extremely useful color for floral design.

The first signs of spring are the yellow-green blossoms of witch hazel and forsythia, which are followed closely by brilliant daffodils in a multitude of yellows. Bringing these glorious blooms into your home is like capturing indoors a breath of spring itself. Summer explodes with a wide range of yellow flowers, such as 'Cherry Drop' gladiolus, black-eyed Susans, 'Moonbeam' coreopsis, 'Pacific Yellow' calendula, 'Rocket' snapdragons, and *Zinnia elegans,* all of which are beautiful in floral designs. Daylilies also offer a range of yellows, from the green-yellow of 'Hyperion' to the golden yellow of 'Evergold'. Our favorite sunflowers for cutting are 'Yellow Disk' and 'Full Sun', which are a deep golden color, and 'Valentine', which is lemon yellow. Dahlias and chrysanthemums, two of Monet's favorites, also make great cutting flowers and are available in an array of yellows.

Vegetables, as well as flowers, can add cheerful yellows to an arrangement. 'Lemon Boy' and 'Yellow Canary' cherry tomatoes provide great texture and color in arrangements. 'Golden Summer' bell peppers, too, bring an unusual touch to an arrangement and are perfect when potted.

The variations of yellow from cool to warm make it invaluable in creating beautiful color movement within a design. Group cool and warm yellows together and then mix in bright reds or deep violets. This variety of tones creates an enchanting color display within the design.

Gloriosa daisies offer an amazing range of cheerful yellows, some even tending toward orange. The pleasing contrasts of velvety blacks and browns provided by their centers make them particularly beautiful in floral designs.

Daylilies in a gentle

shade of apricot and a

deep rusty orange mix

well with gladiolus in

pinks and yellows as well

as a flaming orange.

White phlox and the

lacy foliage of fringed

bleeding heart make a

creative filler.

Orange

Orange is a bright and sometimes garish color when used alone. Most people either love it or hate it. Looking at orange in its variations from light to dark, we see apricot, tangerine, and burnt orange. In red-orange we have salmon, poppy, and hot orange. When taken to its darkest extreme, orange becomes brown.

The color orange and most of its variations couple well with yellow and red. Indeed, Monet's restored garden at Giverny uses these colors to create "sunset borders," for Monet positioned these orange, yellow, and red blooms in an area of his garden where the setting sun would intensify their tones and make them shine even more brilliantly, like molten lava pouring from a volcano. Van Gogh, too, loved orange and yellow, particularly in combination with black.

Red

Red is a primary color, and is flanked by orange and violet on the color wheel. Like yellow, red is very well represented in the floral world, offering great opportunities for interesting color display. Because of the variety of tints, shades, and tones within this one hue, it is a favorite for use in monochromatic color harmonies. Red is the boldest of all the colors, and from it we derive pink, scarlet, ruby, and crimson, while a combination of violet and red renders rose pink, cerise, and maroon.

Favorite red flowers for arrangements include tulips, which appear in a wide range of colors beginning with florists' stock in February and extending through April, when the bulbs bloom in the garden. 'Angelique' is a very romantic blush pink peony tulip that makes an excellent cut flower. Lily-flowered, cottage, and dramatic bicolor tulips round out the possibilities for tulips, and make selecting blossoms akin to a child's visit to a candy store.

Roses, which range from the palest pink 'Eden' to the deepest crimson 'Othello', are also significant in the family of reds. The Pacific Giant series of delphiniums includes a color selection called 'Astotat', which features shades ranging from blush to lilac-pink to deep raspberry rose. Peonies, too, contribute rosy color as well as lush flower form with cultivars such as 'Sarah Bernhardt', a delicate pale pink peony with blooms that look like giant scoops of ice cream. 'Bowl of Beauty' is a scarlet peony with the bonus of a bright golden center.

Garden annuals, biennials, and perennials offer a huge selection of colorful varieties throughout the growing season. Poppies, pink coneflowers, astilbe, sweet Williams, cosmos, snapdragons, and zinnias are all excellent cut flowers that come in dazzling shades of red.

Red is also well represented in the kitchen garden, and many vegetable varieties add interest to a floral arrangement. We particularly enjoy using red runner bean blossoms and red rainbow chard, and take full advantage of ornamental cabbage and kale for late autumn arrangements. And don't overlook bushes and shrubs that can add reds to an arrangement; winterberry, red-twig dogwood, and rose hips all make beautiful textural accents.

Red's complementary color is green, and a combination of these two colors makes for one of the most dramatic harmonies. Most often, red and green arrangements are associated with holiday displays, which make good use of holly, pine, and poinsettias.

Red seems to have more gradations—tints, tones, and shades—than any other color. We use them all as often as possible by looking beyond the cutting garden for deep scarlet berries, leaves, and twigs to use in arrangements throughout the year. These rose hips, crabapples, and holly berries will add color to arrangements from autumn through winter.

57

COLOR

Right: Carolyn gathers a bunch of purple lark-spur from the garden in front of our guest cot-tage. Violet and blue are two colors with very subtle gradations— sometimes the difference between the two hues is barely discernable. Opposite: This arrange-ment of cornflowers, blue salvia, and sweet peas is set off by a brown earthenware crock. Clay brown serves as a good neutral container color for natural-looking bouquets.

Violet

Violet is made up of red and blue. A romantic color, it is especially popular in creating Victorian themes. Violet encompasses pale shades, often referred to as lavender or lilac, and deeper tones such as plum. It may also have a blue tint—an addition that produces a rich violet-blue color—and the transition from true violet to true blue is almost imperceptible.

The most important flower in the violet spectrum is the Japanese iris; its red-violet and blue-violet blossoms are irresistibly dramatic options for arrangements. Wild fennel, small globe thistle (*Echinops ritro*), anemone, *Lisianthus*, and 'Marine' ox-eyes offer additional flower choices in this delicate color. Sprigs of lavender, sweet violet blossoms, and 'Sterling Silver' roses offer the arranger the beauty of romantic color along with delightful fragrance.

Nor should the vegetable garden be neglected when you are gathering material for a violet-colored arrangement—garlic chive flower heads, eggplants, and purple grapes are excellent additions to floral designs. The fruits of wayside plants such as pokeweed and elderberry can also add textural interest. Violet is shown to best effect in monochromatic color harmonies or when grouped with blooms in orange, its complementary color.

Blue

Blue is a primary color, and is a component of green (when combined with yellow) and violet (when mixed with red). Blue is the one color that seems to stay cool, no matter which tint, tone, or shade is used. Although there are fewer flowers to choose from in the blue range than in other color ranges, those blue blossoms we do have make exceptional additions to floral designs.

Irises offer the largest selection of blues, many of which lean strongly toward blue-violet. Blue roses, such as 'Blue Girl' and 'Blueberry Hill', supply a tinge of color but contribute more novelty than true splashes of blue to arrangements. Delphiniums, larkspur, blue salvia, 'Blue Horizon' ageratum, and 'Blue Barlow' columbine offer a good selection of cut flowers for the arranger. Our favorite blue, however, is 'Heavenly Blue' morning glory. Cut when the first blossom on a long vine opens, this climber makes the most spectacular addition to an arrange-ment—every day a new flower opens in a different place.

Blues are best coupled with yellow, their complement—together these hues create truly stunning floral designs. Blue is also a very important color in combination with pinks and mauves when a triadic or polychromatic color theme is your goal.

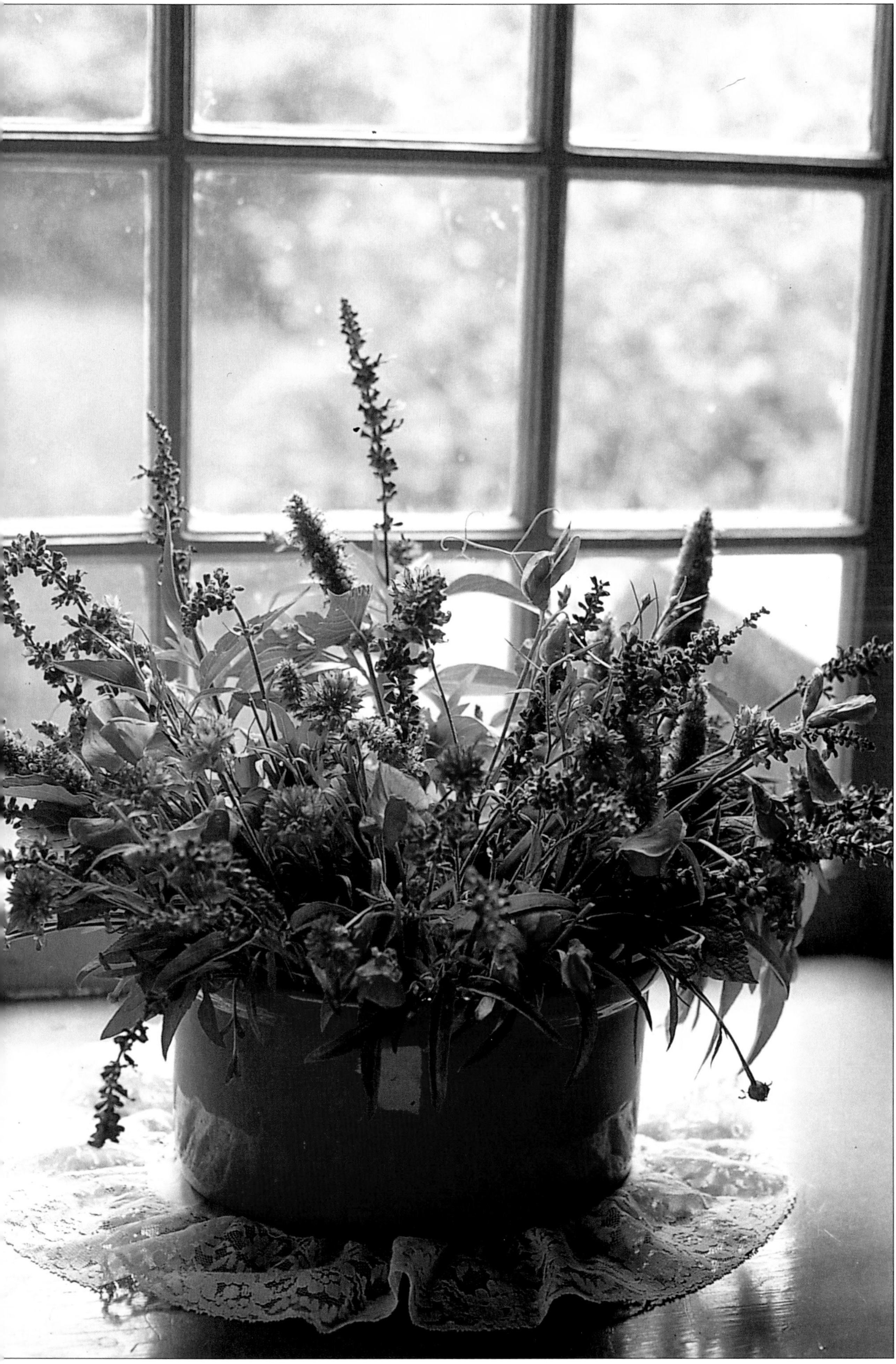

CHAPTER 5

Containers

"The glasses (thirty-two in all) themselves

are beautiful, nearly all are white, clear and

pure, with a few pale green and paler rose and

delicate blue, one or two of richer pink, all

brilliantly clear and filled with absolutely

colorless water…"

Celia Thaxter,

An Island Garden

Rose bowls were favorite containers from the early 1930s through the 1940s; these glass containers were covered by removable lids that had holes to keep stems in place. Today they are prized finds at flea markets. Shown here displaying a choice selection of daffodils, our rose bowl is used to hold many kinds of flowers.

This papier-mâché green bucket will not hold water, but a simple plastic liner is all that's needed to transform it into a useful container for cut flowers. Vessels such as this are lightweight, but can be made to look like they are cast from heavier material with the addition of decorative paint.

For our purposes, a container is any object that holds water and has room for flowers (although if you are using dried flowers, it needn't even hold water). The smallest container we use at Cedaridge Farm is a tiny bud vase, in which we display a single miniature rose. The biggest "container" we own is an antique sleigh we found in the barn when we moved to Cedaridge. We pull it from the barn every Christmas and fill it to overflowing with gift-wrapped parcels and holly boughs bright with berries. Your choices for containers are limited only by your imagination. Once you've started collecting containers, we assure you that the search for new and unusual ones never ends.

CHOOSING A SHAPE AND SIZE

A container for fresh flowers can be in any shape and of any size and material, providing it can be made waterproof. The most popular containers are generally taller then they are wide and have substantial bases to ensure that the arrangements do not topple over. The ginger-jar design, which has a neck that is smaller than the center of the container, is a particularly useful form. Stems are held upright by the neck rim, and the bottoms of the stems rest securely against the sides of the jar. Because of the jar's shape, there is usually no need for added inside support.

In addition to the size and shape of the container, don't forget to consider the vessel's material. You may even choose to disguise the container completely with vines, bark, fabric, or other materials, and thus the container that actually holds the flowers can be any old pot, pail, or plastic tub.

MATCHING CONTAINERS WITH FLOWERS
AND LOCATIONS

Containers should furnish the link between the arrangement's raison d'être, its contents, and the location in which it is placed. Some containers are associated with particular flowers and locations: long, slender glass vases, flared at the top, are perfect for displaying long-stemmed roses on windowsills.

Baskets, crocks, and old coffeepots evoke images of simple country life and are perfect for displaying sprigs of lavender, long-stemmed poppies, and nodding daisies. Seashore plants like sea holly, Kingfisher daisies, and Carolina lupines are most at home in vessels expressive of the ocean—try cauldrons, seashells, and nautical buckets. A porcelain jardinière may conjure up memories of a family trip to Provence as well as serve as a lovely container.

Glass and Crystal

Even though stems seen through clear glass containers can be attractive and, in fact, may be part of the overall design, the water in the container must be clear at all times. Although it is advisable to change the water often for the general benefit of the flowers, the right choice of flowers for a glass container is also important. Some flowers, such as daffodils and hollyhocks, exude a milky substance that clouds the water, thus making a clear container a high-maintainance choice. On the other hand, contorted branches like apple twigs and grape vines can be dramatic when viewed in the depths of the vase, adding texture and line below the floral display. These branches also give support to the smaller or weaker stems in the arrangement.

Location is important when deciding whether or not to use a clear vase. If the background is of special interest—perhaps a beautiful wallpaper or a colorful antique screen—and will show through the container from behind, the resulting composition can be breathtaking.

Rose bowls—dishlike containers with low bases and glass lids that have holes to support stiff stems—first became popular in the 1930s and 1940s. The woody stems of roses do not discolor the water, and the perforated lid firmly holds the head of each rose, creating an especially beautiful display when the flowers are at the height of bloom. Although these containers have become scarce, it is a special treat to find a good example in an antique shop. Rose bowls can also be used to display other strong-stemmed flowers, such as daffodils and zinnias.

Cut crystal vases are a special pleasure to work with because often only a few stems are needed to produce an elegant display. Let a simple design be your goal, allowing the container to be the main attraction. Cut crystal vases can be expensive but will stand on their own as decorative pieces.

Colored glass is an interesting possibility, though it can look garish unless the contents, container, and location are carefully related. As with clear glass, the stems should not detract from the overall design, though this is less of a problem with colored glass because the stems are normally less visible. The selection of vase color is a very personal choice, but take care that the color does not overwhelm or compete with the blooms. Pressed glass in various shades was manufactured throughout the Depression era and can still be found at flea markets, not to mention Grandmother's attic. These soft pinks and greens, as well as ambers and amethysts, give a beautiful, old-fashioned flair to arrangements. Victorian pressed glass vases and bowls, too, are favorite collectibles, though rather more expensive than pieces manufactured later. While colored glass from the Victorian era is available in many colors, cranberry remains the most popular; these shades are generally quite rich and are best suited to opulent arrangements.

White and Black Containers

Although white and black might seem to be the most neutral container colors, you must take special care when using these colors to create a perfect union between contents, container, and location. White is a conspicuous color; it jumps out and draws attention away from other colors around it. One way to use a white container successfully is to make the contents predominately white, adding other colors—such as pink, blue, or yellow—like frosting.

Black—the opposite of white—tends to recede, and it can subdue bright colors. Black used in large clumps also gives the appearance of holes. To complement a black container, choose bright-colored, densely packed flowers; blooms with black centers, such as sunflowers, will set off a black container. Charcoal gray twigs such as those from plum trees or curly willows are an excellent choice for use in a black container, as the tracery of branches provides an extension of color.

Beautifully crafted and often expensive crystal containers such as this Italian vase are best paired with dramatic flowers, like the Aurelian hybrid lilies pictured here.

In two favorite old cof-

feepots, branches of

early-flowering white

servistree and red quince

adorn the sunroom at

Cedaridge Farm.

Layering containers by

placing one of the coffee-

pots inside a large bas-

ket adds interest to the

overall display.

Pottery, Crocks, and Porcelain

If we tried to detail all the containers in this group, the list would be endless, but pottery and porcelain of every description offer good potential as containers. Although most often thought of as a choice for country or informal arrangements, crockery can also make successful containers for traditional and formal displays. Of particular appeal are clay and terra-cotta pots.

Baskets

Flowers can look fabulous in baskets. The trick is to choose baskets that are special in texture or shape. The most desirable baskets for flowers are made from the pliable stems of willow and grapevine, rather than "strawmarket" raffia and reed, which tend to look flimsy. Always be on the lookout for unusual shapes, vintage baskets, or ones that have been painted and repainted, all of which can add special charm to your arrangements. Even baskets intended for wastepaper can look fabulous when filled with tall lupines, hollyhocks, and delphiniums. Look for square, tall, or even disk-shaped baskets—all can make an arrangement unique.

Baskets do require the addition of a watertight liner if used for fresh flower arranging. Because the basket hides the liner, it needn't be stylish or expensive. Even plastic gallon milk cartons with the tops cut away are functional as watertight inner receptacles.

Bowls, Boards, and Trays

Bowls are the basic shallow containers appropriate for tabletop or centerpiece arrangements in the mass or all-around style. They can be made of almost any material but are usually glass, plastic, or ceramic. Your local crafts store or florist shop is sure to have a good selection of flower bowls. With low sides and a wide top, a bowl can hold a great many flowers without needing to be built up high. When working with a bowl, however, it is almost always necessary to use some mechanical form (such as Oasis or a grid constructed of wire or adhesive tape) to hold the flowers in position. Clear fish bowls and opaque mixing bowls (especially collectable ones like yellowware and McCoy) also make attractive containers. Experiment with unusual "bowls," such as antique butter dishes, wash basins, wooden salad bowls, and even shaving mugs.

Boards do not have sides and are most often used in still-life arrangements; the arrangement is assembled directly on the board. Dried or fresh flowers and an object compatible with the theme of the arrangement, such as a bird, butterfly, or ceramic statue, are then added.

Trays are flat and have shallow, raised edges. They can range from expensive silver pieces to throwaway plastic ones. Trays are most often used in line style arrangements, using a pinholder secured by adhesive clay to hold the arrangement. Bonsai dishes are special traylike containers that are particularly appropriate for Oriental arrangements.

SOURCES

Containers are available from many sources: flea markets, yard sales, and odds-and-ends shops often yield unusual collectibles and sometimes even valuable pieces. Antiques stores and auctions are good sources for charming vintage items such as antique silver trophy cups, Victorian bowl-and-pitcher sets, and elaborate crystal and cut glass vases.

The glasswares section of your local hardware store is especially useful, generally stocking mugs, glasses, pitchers, bowls, trays, and pots of all shapes, sizes, and price ranges. The hardware store is also likely to have wooden tubs and metal pails in a variety of sizes. Particularly useful are ash buckets of a size that can be filled to overflowing with masses of daffodils, roses, or asters.

As you might expect, the garden center is also an excellent source of creative containers. Flowerpots, window boxes, and urns are made in every shape, size, and material imaginable. Don't overlook wheelbarrows and carts for holding larger arrangements, especially on holiday occasions like Thanksgiving and Christmas.

Look around your backyard, garage, and porch, as well as throughout the house, and you will suddenly discover many objects to convert into attractive and useful containers.

Whatever the occasion and whichever container you choose, a little thought and creative energy are sure to result in an arrangement that adds unique charm to your home.

Large crocks and pieces of pottery, old coffeepots, baskets, and stylized collectible vases are among the containers we've accumulated. Our extensive collection allows us to create lovely arrangements for every room in the house throughout the course of the year.

67

CONTAINERS

CHAPTER 6

Structure

"I try to grasp what is essential—later I fill in

the spaces which are bounded by contours—

either expressed or not, but in any case *felt*."

Vincent van Gogh

in a letter to his brother Theo

A natural-looking mass of azaleas is accented by a collar
of lilacs and a few slender stalks of lily-of-the-valley.

Structure is the architecture of an arrangement. A simple dome of zinnias has structure, but structure is most obvious in large arrangements that use sinuous branches and arching grasses to bring visual excitement to the composition.

Begin thinking about the structure of an arrangement as you choose the contents, which can be divided into four groups: line material, main material, filler material, and accent material.

LINE MATERIAL

Line material is made up of long elements—flowering spikes such as delphinium, larkspur, gladiolus, long-stemmed roses in bud, and fragrant hosta flowers; curly branches such as contorted willow, crape myrtle, or witch hazel; greens such as tall ostrich fern; and pod heads on long stems from plants such as Siberian iris, blackberry lily, and milkweed. This line material is used to create the outline or determine the shape of the arrangement. In a mass arrangement, line material defines the edges; in a line arrangement, it is often the focal point of the design, particularly in asymmetrical arrangements. In the line-mass style, the tall material also penetrates beyond the central mass of the arrangement, creating the exterior limit or fading into space.

MAIN MATERIAL

The main material is the most obvious element of the arrangement and is often used as reference, as in "the bright pink zinnia arrangement" or "the delicate rose arrangement." Usually, the flowers used as main material are rounded, are full-bodied, or in clusters and are in dramatic colors: lilies, roses in full bloom, peonies, and hydrangeas are perfect choices for main material. Dramatic foliage is also useful as the main material; frilly ornamental kale, golden-edged hosta leaves, and prickly variegated holly make striking main material.

FILLER MATERIAL

Filler material is traditionally used to close the spaces between blossoms in an arrangement. Sometimes, filling these voids and spaces can detract from the energy in an arrangement, making it look stuffed and boring. Baby's breath, florist fern, and asparagus fern are commonly used filler material, but they tend to make an arrangement look dull and unimaginative. More creative filler material are pink love grass, with its airy, delicate sprays; lemony sprigs of lady's mantle flowers; and blue forget-me-nots, with their twinkling yellow eyes. To be different, you can also use filler as a base, first rimming the container with it, then adding main and accent flowers.

Main material is usually the "name" of the arrangement, such as a rose arrangement or a lily arrangement. Although full-bodied flowers most often serve as main material, any blossom or foliage shape that satisfies the design may be used.

Filler material is used to connect the different elements in the design or to provide added dimension. In this arrangement, delicate lady's mantle softens the edge of the container and adds important color to the overall design. These tiny yellow-green flower clusters balance the blowsy, old-fashioned peonies.

A little experimenting will show you when to fill and how much fill you should use. Searching seed catalogs for new kinds of filler material is great fun, and you'll feel gratified as you discover unusual plants that fill your arrangements beautifully while lending them a singular look.

Accent material can be any flower or object that completes the design by providing added dimension. The best accents are subtle, surprising without being glaring. The perfect accent may be one bright flower, a few pine cones, fruit, berries, vegetables, or even a bird's nest. Choosing the right accent material while taking into account the proper amount and most striking placement is an important facet of the the art of arranging flowers.

ACCENT MATERIAL

Accent material makes the arrangement memorable. It can be as simple as one red tulip in a mass of lilac blossoms, a bunch of star-shaped coreopsis in a hot color arrangement, or a lone pine cone in an arrangement of chrysanthemums.

Because accents carry a great amount of visual weight, they work especially well in the lower central sections of the arrangements. Accents can drip over the edge of the container, extending beyond the basic arrangement and penetrating its surroundings. Accents also aid in the development of a strong line, whether diagonal, vertical, or horizontal. Objects lying on a table were the favored accents of the French Impressionists in their still-life paintings. Cézanne often used peaches, apples, and onions, as well as sinister skulls and sensual conch shells, as embellishments in his floral still lifes. Renoir and van Gogh used the more traditional approach of flowers strewn at the base of the arrangement.

BUILDING THE ARRANGEMENT

Before you begin arranging flowers, find a space where you can work comfortably. The size of the space you select is, of course, directly related to the volume of arranging you can do. If you plan to arrange only occasionally, with flowers bought from a florist or farmer's market, the kitchen sink will do. However, if you grow flowers in your garden and plan to arrange flowers frequently, give yourself a special area in which to work. You will need a table and some shelves or benches to hold your containers. As your collection grows, you might find it convenient to group them by style or material, placing glass vases and bowls in one area, baskets in another, and so on. Organizing your containers not only saves the time you would spend searching all over the house for a specific piece, seeing them together helps you select the right container for the job.

The table you choose to work on does not need to be large but should always be clear of any other objects. We prefer a surface at counter height (about forty inches [102cm]), with high stools that allow us to sit comfortably and view our work closely.

Next to the containers we situate the buckets of conditioned flowers, placing them so that every blossom is in view. You will need easy access to a deep sink with running water. Water is the life support system of flowers. Be sure your water source can supply both hot and cold water, allowing you to mix or choose the temperature needed for gathering, conditioning, and cleaning. If you do a lot of arranging or if you design floral displays for special events such as weddings and large parties, you might consider checking the pH of your water. If possible, you might consider diverting the water you use for flowers before it passes through your softening system. Salinity and fluoride can both adversely affect the longevity of cut flowers.

Once the flowers have been gathered from the garden or purchased from the garden center or florist, it is time to choose a style, shape, and expression for your arrangement. Usually, you know what kind of arrangement you want before you select the flowers, but sometimes an idea arises spontaneously as you gather a bouquet. Often, the container you want to use helps determine the style; at other times, the season or the intended location for the arrangement are deciding factors.

Once you have chosen a container, determine what you will need to hold the flowers in place. Often, you can avoid using a mechanical device entirely by weaving the stems of the first five or six flowers into a network. This gives the arrangement the most natural feeling and cuts down on the amount of supplies you need to keep on hand. If the arrangement does require a mechanical holder, our first choice is crumpled chicken wire, since the holes offer support but still allow the stems to be ruled by gravity and look natural. Our least favorite holder is Oasis, because it can restrict the flowers, holding them too firmly. Oasis is preferred, however, when you are using a valuable container, such as a silver wine cooler, that can be scratched by chicken wire.

Decide the shape of the arrangement—triangular, vertical, or horizontal—and add the line material to outline the shape. It is important at this stage to determine the desired height and width of the final arrangement. By creating this outline at the beginning, you'll find it easier to judge balance and the creative process will flow more smoothly.

Always keep in mind the setting for the arrangement and the distance from which it will be viewed. This information is vital in deciding the colors and shapes you will use. A small end table arrangement, which will be viewed at a close range from the chair beside it, can contain smaller flowers than an arrangement intended for the end of a long hallway, where bold, bright colors will be necessary to create visual impact.

The glass-topped table in our sunroom is a convenient spot to examine flowers before we arrange them. Discard any flowers with broken petals or weak stems, and remove leaves that will fall below the water line.

75

STRUCTURE

Once you've established the outline, add the main materials, being careful to keep different colors and shapes on different planes, placing darker colors deep within the arrangement and allowing lighter, brighter colors to radiate out from the center. Be sure to use all stages of flower life: a combination of tight buds, mature buds, and fully opened flowers adds interest and makes the arrangement look alive.

When adding flowers as filler material, be sure that the fill is actually necessary. Bunching a few flowers together to create an informal mass often looks better than small, fussy filler material.

Leaving space between the flowers is essential. Clutter makes a confusing design. Foliage also plays an important role in a design, and it is best to use the foliage of the flowers rather than something totally foreign, unless the different foliage has been added as an accent or for textural interest.

As you work, step back to look at your arrangement from time to time. The building of an arrangement is a step-by-step process; each flower balances with those previously added.

Consider carefully the rhythm and balance of the overall design before determining the placement of accent flowers. Position them to reflect a movement within the design; this will lend definition to the overall composition.

Learn when to stop. Overstuffing the arrangement results in a displeasing design. A beautifully curving branch with a few accent flowers is much more exciting than a vase crammed with blooms.

For this summery arrangement we chose a hot color harmony and linked it thematically with a lobster feast. We selected the lard crock for its earthy look. Before we began arranging, we filled the container with rolled chicken wire to hold the stems in place.

1 Deep rose and red-orange Asiatic lilies serve as both line and main material. Grouping them close to the center, we are careful to position them in a relaxed manner so they do not look stiff. Placing these darker flowers at the center will give the finished arrangement a greater sense of depth.

2 Next, we add a few yellow lilies. We've left their stems a bit longer than those of the red lilies to allow them to gracefully lean toward the edge of the container. This addition completes the general outline of the design. To add more color, we elect to leave the stamens intact.

3 For contrasting shape, we add two or three gloriosa daisies, tucking them in among both hues of lilies.

4 Several stems of 'Moonbeam' coreopsis are bunched together and added to the design as filler material.

5 The completed arrangement, with freshly cooked lobsters.

When building your arrangement, consider the location and surrounding materials, as "harmony" extends beyond the individual design. This vibrant display of summer annuals is complemented by the basket of red 'Titan' raspberries.

CREATING AN ARRANGEMENT

These step-by-step instructions will guide you in creating an arrangement, from start to finish.

- Find a place to work. You should have a flat surface on which to place the container and enough space to assemble all supplies, containers, and buckets of cut flowers.
- Determine the style of the arrangement, fitting it to the occasion.
- Choose the line, main, filler, and accent materials, being sure all have been properly conditioned.
- Choose the container and prepare any mechanical support, such as chicken wire or Oasis.
- Add warm water and floral preservative to the container. If the container is large, fill it only halfway with water to facilitate moving the arrangement into its final location.
- Place line material first to "outline" the arrangement.
- Add the main material to create the body of the arrangement, being sure to give each flower enough space. Do not repeat shapes or colors on the same plane.
- Step back from the arrangement frequently to check balance, rhythm, and color harmony. Always keep in mind the distance between the finished arrangement and the viewer.
- Decide whether any filler will be necessary.
- Add accent material—an element of surprise is the secret to a memorable design.
- Stop when the design has reached proportions that are pleasing to your eye. Be careful of any tendency to overfill, because it will ultimately weaken your design.
- When the arrangement is complete, place it in its viewing position. Check that it is not in a draft, direct sunlight, or deep shadow and that it is not obscured by an object blocking it from view.
- Top off the container with water.
- Clean your work area of clipped stems and discarded flowers. Wipe clippers and return all supplies to their storage area. Empty buckets, wash them thoroughly with soapy water, and rinse with bleach.

CHAPTER 7

Conditioning

"I go forth between five and six o'clock to

cut them...taking a tall slender pitcher...and

as I cut each stem dropping the flower...so

that the stem is covered nearly its whole

length with water. Gathered in this way they

have no opportunity to lose their freshenss."

Celia Thaxter

on harvesting poppies

Larkspur, asters, and cornflowers gathered from the garden will become
beautiful floral arrangements filling the rooms at Cedaridge Farm.

Beautiful mixed bouquets make exquisite gifts and are great fun to arrange as they are gathered in the garden. Be sure to remove any thorns and excess leaves before placing the pre-arranged bunch of flowers in a bucket of warm water. Leave the bouquet in a cool area for a few hours before wrapping for presentation.

aking the time to condition flowers properly is an essential part of building a lasting floral arrangement. Not all flowers are conditioned by the same methods, and it is important to learn the differences to ensure the most successful, long-lasting displays. Gathering blooms from the garden at a favorable time also helps to lengthen their vase life.

CUTTING FLOWERS FROM THE GARDEN

Flowers cut from the garden for fresh flower arrangements should be cut in the early morning or in the late evening, when they contain the most natural moisture. Avoid cutting flowers for fresh arrangements in the middle of the day or when it is hot and sunny, when flowers are most drained of moisture and energy. (Flowers cut for drying, however, should be gathered on a sunny, dry day in the middle of the afternoon, when they contain the least amount of moisture [see Chapter 9]).

Carry a bucket containing a small amount of warm water with you into the garden, adding each stem to the water as soon as it is cut. Make sure the bottom of the stem reaches the water.

When cutting from the garden, look for straight stems, cutting as much length as possible. If your arrangement calls for some short stems, take two buckets with you and divide the cuttings by length, giving each blossom enough room so it is not crowded, pinched, or mashed as others are added. Remove excess leaves quickly and plunge stems into the water. Leaves can deteriorate quickly when submerged in water (also emitting an unpleasant putrid odor), so you should remove them as soon as the flower is cut.

In any given planting, the quality of flowers' shape, form, and color can vary considerably. For example, some flowers have weak heads, which makes them arch appealingly, but others may be blemished from disease or stress, which spoils the crisp, clean, healthy look of an arrangement. Pay particular attention to variegated foliage—unless the variegation is clean and obvious it can look anemic, as though the plant is suffering from poor nutrition or lack of light. Choosing good shape and form and interesting color aids greatly in each individual flower's clarity. Flowers must also have good color intensity —even white and pastel shades—if they are to be appealing in an arrangement.

Learn the merits of flowers you grow for cutting. In general, annuals and perennials should be cut when freshly open but most bulbs, such as tulips, daffodils, and gladiolus, are best cut when only half open or just as they begin to show color. Flowering fruit tree branches should be cut when the bud first shows color.

There are, however, several exceptions to this rule. Tall spiky flowers, such as delphiniums, larkspurs, snapdragons, stocks, lupines, and lilies-of-the valley are best cut when the lower florets

You can glimpse the

flower garden at

Cedaridge Farm beyond

the entrance to the conser-

atory. A good reason to

have a cutting garden

close to the house is the

luxury of having fresh

flowers for long-lasting

arrangements.

are freshly opened and the upper florets are still in bud. Daylilies can be cut any time after the first flower has opened. Although each blossom lasts only a day, the remaining flowers on the stalk will generally bloom one day at a time. Bearded irises are much the same, especially the repeat bloomers that flower in late spring and again in late summer. Once the first flower has bloomed, cutting the stem will not deter the other buds from opening.

Many good flowers are overlooked as cutting material—especially those of flowering annual vines. Morning glory is a good example. Choosing a long section of vine with many buds, we cut it after the first blossom has opened. Placing the stem in deep water (not Oasis, as it cannot draw enough water), the flowers will continue to bloom one day at a time, often for a week or more, depending on the number of buds on the vine. Every morning a new flower is blooming—but in a different part of the arrangement! Chicory is another example of a somewhat neglected flower. The beautiful, soft blue, star-shaped flowers lining the tall stems are only open in the morning, closing to tight knots by noon. Plan to use them in an arrangement for your breakfast table to be sure you don't miss their bloom time.

CONDITIONING CUT FLOWERS

When a flower stem is cut, it immediately begins to protect itself, closing its pores to help retain the moisture in its cells. Conditioning, or hardening, is a necessary procedure that ensures that as much water as possible is absorbed by the flower before it completely seals off its pores. If a flower is not conditioned, but rather placed directly into a vase after it is cut, the bloom will begin to wilt within a short period of time.

Taking the time to properly condition flowers is, therefore, an essential part of building a lasting floral arrangement. Most flowers can be conditioned quite easily. Place them in a bucket of warm water, submerging the stems all the way to the flower head, and leave them in a cool, dark location for several hours or overnight. Adding floral preservative at this time gives the flowers a chance to absorb essential sugar. Also, a few drops of household bleach added to the water aids in slowing the growth of bacteria.

But not all flowers are conditioned by the same methods, and it is important to learn the differences to ensure the most successful long-lasting displays.

Tulips

Tulips are unique in that they continue to grow after the stem has been cut from the bulb. This is often referred to as wilting, but in fact, the stem is growing and will seek out the area with the most light. Creative floral designers will take advantage of this natural characteristic and plan for the graceful curves. Tulips also require a bit more attention in the conditioning process than other flowers.

1. The white part at the bottom of the stem should be cut away—it does not draw water. Be sure to cut the stem at an angle—this prevents the bottom of the stem from resting flat on the bottom of the container, reducing the amount of water intake.

2. Tulips do not like floral preservatives added to the water.

3. Wrap the cut flowers in damp paper (newspaper will do) covering the head, but exposing about a third of the stem.

4. Place the bundle in a container half filled with warm water and let it soak for about eight hours. Make sure the flower heads are not below the water.

While daffodils should not be mixed in an arrangement with other types of flowers because of the gluey substance they produce, we've cheated a bit in this arrangement by putting the daffodils in a small glass and adding the young maple leaves to the water in the mug. This container within a container effectively separates the daffodils from the woody-stemmed maple, allowing both plants maximum water intake.

5. Remove the flowers from the water, but do not remove the paper. Lay the bundle in a cool area, away from any draft or direct sunlight, until you are ready to arrange.

6. Tulips are heavy drinkers. Do not arrange them in Oasis, as they cannot then draw the water they need.

Daffodils

Once cut, daffodils exude a viscous substance that can block the water intake of other flowers. Tulips, because they are such heavy drinkers, are especially affected by the contamination of water by daffodils. It is best, therefore, to arrange daffodils solo. If you feel compelled to combine them with other fresh flowers, condition the daffodils first in a bleach solution (five to seven drops of bleach to one quart [950ml] of water) for three to four hours. Rinse stems before arranging the flowers.

Daffodils, unlike tulips, should be conditioned and stored in very shallow water, as totally submerged daffodil stems deteriorate very quickly.

Poppies, Dahlias, Hollyhocks, and Balloon Flowers

These flowers all exude a milky sap upon being cut. This sap immediately coagulates as the plant tries to protect itself from losing moisture. Holding a match, candle, or lighter to the cut stem for a few seconds will stop the sap from running and will prevent the feeding cells from closing. Once this is done, place the flowers in a bucket of warm water and keep them in a cool area for several hours until you are ready to arrange them.

Stocks, Violets, and Lilies-of-the-Valley

This group of flowers prefers to be arranged with their "boots" on. Instead of cutting the stems, pull these flowers up by their roots. Simply shake the soil away, rinse the roots so that they don't contaminate the water, and condition them like any other flowers—in a bucket of warm water placed in a cool location for several hours.

Woody-Stemmed Plants

Lilacs, rhododendrons, forsythia, quince, hawthorn, and any other woody-stemmed plants need more of the stem exposed than the cut bottom to ensure that they can get the water they need to remain fresh. Strip away the bark about two inches (5cm) from the bottom of the stem and make one or two vertical slits to open the stem. Though some books recommend smashing the ends of the stems with a hammer, we don't like this method because we believe it damages the cells, interfering with the intake of water. Submerge as much of the stem as possible in a bucket of warm water and leave in a cool area for several hours before arranging.

Woody-stemmed plants should not be arranged in Oasis, as they cannot absorb the water they need to remain fresh.

Wildflowers

Wildflowers are notoriously difficult to condition with success, as they are usually somewhat fragile and short-lived once collected. We have found that conditioning for wildflowers is hit-or-miss, and success depends on the life cycle of the flower, the amount of moisture in the air, and many other ill-defined and unpredictable circumstances.

A small table on the balcony overlooking the gardens at Cedaridge Farm is perfect for holding a gathering of flowers. With proper conditioning and aftercare, the flowers continue to look fresh day after day.

When working with wildflowers, be selective and cut only what you will be sure to use. The rest are best enjoyed in the garden.

REVIVING WILTED FLOWERS

When you buy your flowers at a florist, some time may elapse before you arrive home, and the flowers may look rather wilted from the heat of the car. Remarkably, you can revive the flowers by submersing them for a minute or two in nearly boiling water.

1. Cut about one inch (2.5cm) from the bottom of the stem, working at an angle.
2. Protect the flower heads with a collar of paper or with a paper bag.
3. Place the stems in water that is simmering, not boiling, and hold them in place for a minute or two.
4. Remove the paper collar and place the flowers in a bucket of warm water up to the flower heads. Leave them to soak for eight hours or overnight. This treatment is also beneficial because it kills bacteria, which will considerably shorten the life of the flowers if allowed to grow unchecked.

Another remarkable treatment for reviving flowers involves submerging them completely, head and stems, in a tub of tepid water. Place a weight, such as a brick or dish, on the stems close to the head to keep the flowers from floating. Within a few hours, the flowers will be perky. Using this method we have even revived roses that dropped onto the lawn and were run over by the tires of a rider mower!

Clusters of miniature

roses grouped with a few

white phlox in a glass

vase create a charming

arrangement among the

toys in a child's bedroom.

ARRANGEMENT AFTERCARE

Here are a few simple steps you can take to maximize the life of your arrangement.

- Check water level daily, changing whenever possible. Top off large arrangements that are difficult to move.
- Remove any faded or dead blossoms from day bloomers like daylilies and morning glories.
- Remove any wilted flowers and replace them if you expect the arrangement to be in position for any length of time.
- Wipe any pollen that may have fallen on the tabletop or linens beneath the arrangement.
- Remove the arrangement *before* it has faded.
- Compost or discard the contents, wash the container with soapy water, and rinse it with bleach. Dry it and return it to the storage area.

Location

"Opening out on the long piazza over the

flower beds, and extending almost its whole

length, runs the large, light, airy room…the high

walls to the ceiling are covered with pictures, and

flowers are everywhere."

Celia Thaxter,

An Island Garden

*Because it is brightly lit by two angled windows that provide almost
all-around light, the corner of a sunroom at Cedaridge Farm is the
ideal location for arrangements of potted flowering bulbs.*

ocations for flower arrangements are chosen for a variety of reasons but most often to address a need in a room; the right arrangement can brighten a space or provide a romantic touch. We may also decorate for a season or for a special event, such as a wedding. Whatever the reason, the final destination of the arrangement is crucial.

To provide the ultimate location for displaying creative flower arrangements, we added this Victorian-style conservatory to our farmhouse.

CREATING SPECIAL SPACES FOR YOUR ARRANGEMENTS

Most people think of designing flower arrangements for locations around their home—especially a bedroom vanity table, a dining room table, a foyer, or even a table on a deck. But few people ever think of creating locations just to display floral arrangements to advantage! At Cedaridge Farm, we have created two such spaces, a gazebo and a sunroom. (This is not a new idea, though—creation of a special wall alcove, called a tokonoma, for the display of flower arrangements is one of the disciplines within ikebana, the Japanese flower arranging aesthetic.)

Before we had these two special areas, we often created arrangements for the house, and though the rooms were made more cheerful by these arrangements, there were inherent problems. First, we own a two-hundred-year-old farmhouse, and the rooms tend to be cozy and small. Consequently, the arrangements needed to be relatively small, and there never seemed to be enough light falling on the flowers except when they were placed on the windowsills, which are eighteen inches (46cm) deep!

Inside the house, our passion for large, exuberant arrangements could not be fully satisfied, but a romantic, Victorian-style gazebo within view of our front door solved this problem. A table in the center of the gazebo happily accommodates even excessively large arrangements, like an explosive collection of fragrant peonies or a design using human-high gladiolus and dinner plate–size dahlias.

Our favorite location for displaying flowers, however, has been our sunroom, a Victorian-style conservatory. The main table and smaller side tables enjoy natural, ambient light, and the setting is tailor-made for highlighting spectacular arrangements, even though we also use the room for reading, eating, and displaying a collection of houseplants.

Unfortunately, building a space specifically for the ideal display of flower arrangements is not always within our means, and so we must learn to fit appropriate floral arrangements into existing locations. Whether we design a space for flower arrangements or flower arrangements for a space, a floral display is incomplete until it is properly placed in its location.

A bouquet of delicate

'Wedding Day' roses

is just the right size and

visual weight to provide

enchanting contrast to

the heavy stand in this

entryway.

For inspiration on good placement of arrangements within the home, we again look to paintings by the American Impressionist Childe Hassam, who often painted flowers arranged by poet Celia Thaxter. Her parlor on Appledore Island, off the coast of Maine, became a favorite subject for Hassam, not only because her flower arrangements were so natural and cheerful but because the location itself was magical. The sunlit room was filled with books, sheet music, a piano, and paintings; in it writers, artists, and musicians loved to gather for stimulating conversation. Through Hassam's still-life watercolors, we experience a fresh and unaffected approach to arranging flowers. Bunches of flowers freshly picked from Celia's small garden were carefully placed in vases—arranged by color or by flower family—each designed to complement a particular area of the parlor. In Hassam's watercolor painting "The Altar and Shrine," he shows thirty-two vases of Shirley poppies, about which Celia wrote, "I begin on the left end of this bookcase....The color gathers softly flushed from snow white at one end, through all rose, pink, cherry, and crimson shades, to the note of darkest red...here and there a few leaves, stalks and buds....The effect of this arrangement is perfectly beautiful."

Although it is important that flowers relate to their location, they need not directly repeat the style of the room. A modern room may benefit from a lush, old-fashioned bouquet, and a vase full of red tulips can add accent color to a monochromatic decor. Color can also change the tone of the room, giving a formal room a relaxed look or an informal room a feeling of refinement. Adding bright yellow daffodils to the table in a dark-paneled library imparts a lighthearted feeling; deep crimson tulips would create a more somber and subdued mood in the same room.

The Entry Hall

The most common location for an arrangement of flowers is the entry hall. Because the entryway provides the first impression a visitor receives, an arrangement placed there should relate well to the space and to the season. Generally, very little time is spent in this area, so the arrangement should deliver its welcoming message instantly. Even if your home does not have a specific entry area, you can create much the same effect by positioning a small table topped with a bouquet just inside the door.

If fresh flowers are not available, use greens or dried flowers instead. Berries and leaves make a dramatic statement, as does a bountiful display of fruits. Warm, vibrant colors and bold designs send the strongest message of welcome. Don't forget fragrance when planning your entrance bouquet, but don't overdo it either; the mere hint of a scent is more appealing than an overpowering fragrance, no matter how pleasant. Often the inclusion of a single fragrant flower—like a hyacinth or tuberose—is enough. Avoid flowers that have a questionable fragrance. Cleome, although beautiful in an arrangement, emits an unpleasant odor in an enclosed space and is best left for outdoor arrangements. Air temperature is important when considering fragrance—don't expect roses to perfume the room in the middle of July when the air conditioner is set at 60°F (16°C).

Avoid using tiny, dainty arrangements in the entryway—delegate these to the niches and corners of other rooms. Flowers for entry halls are best arranged in low, wide-based, substantial containers. Fragile glass vases are too easily swept to the floor by boisterous visiting children or by the sleeve of a coat.

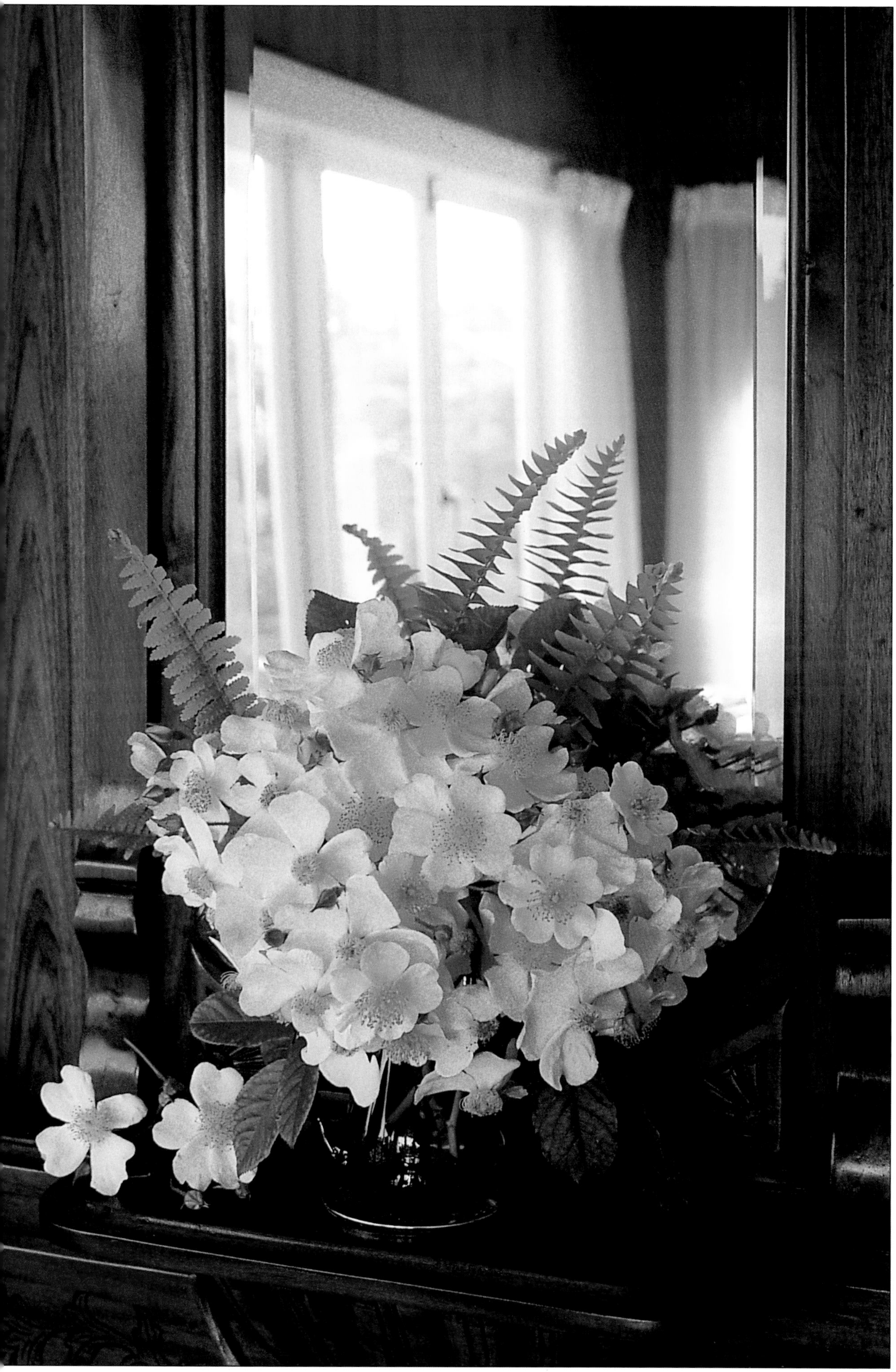

LOCATION

The Living Room

No matter what the decor or the size of the space, the living room can be enhanced with beautiful flowers. Coffee tables and side tables are the most obvious places for arrangements, but don't forget that the space filled with a roaring fire in winter is a black hole the remainder of the year. Remove the screen for the warm months and add a dramatic display of bright flowers or silvery leaves. Dried flowers are an excellent choice for dark areas, as are dried leaves and berries. Keep the colors light and bright, as dark colors such as purples and blues will seem to disappear in shadow.

Corners in many rooms are bare, though they are often in direct view, especially if chairs are placed at an angle. A tall, slender plant stand topped with a beautiful bouquet makes an excellent focal point in the room, softening the corner and creating a perfect location for a year-round display of fresh or dried flowers.

For side tables and coffee tables, keep arrangements small and low so that they don't obstruct the view across the room. Always leave enough space on the table for a teacup or a small book. Letting the arrangement overhang the table or dominate the entire space is a mistake; besides throwing the room off balance by giving too much visual weight to the flowers, the display is likely to be sent crashing to the floor by a careless jostle.

The Dining Room

The dining room is another popular location for flower arrangements, though we must make a distinction between table centerpieces (which must be low enough to look over) and bouquets for the side tables and windows (which can be more extravagant). If flowers are intended as a centerpiece for a dinner party, consider these rules of thumb: first, the arrangement should not be taller than twelve inches (30.5cm), so that guests can talk to each other over the flowers, and second, the centerpiece should be small enough that it can be lifted easily from the table and placed on a nearby shelf or side table should the main table become overcrowded with serving dishes. Arrangements that will be used as centerpieces should follow the dimensions of the table—circular arrangements best suit round and square tables, while long and narrow displays are pleasing on rectangular tables. For very long tables, such as banquet tables, arrangements can be placed every three to five seats, depending on

Opposite: Arrangements look beautiful under paintings. This collection of sea and wind tolerant plants—roses, echinops, baby's breath, poppies, and summer phlox—makes a gorgeous free-flowing arrangement to fill the space under a painting in a seaside cottage.

Left: We always fill the dining room at Cedaridge Farm with fresh flowers from the garden.

Don't forget to include arrangements in every room of your home. Beautiful garden roses are reflected in the dressing table mirror of our bathroom. Here, the color and fragrance are sure to delight you and your family, as well as guests.

the budget and personal preference. Arrangements for the head table should be consistent in style with displays on accompanying tables but may be a bit larger. This larger-size display must still allow diners to view the other guests.

Table centerpieces for the home reflect the lifestyle of the family. Dinner guests provide the perfect excuse for gathering the best flowers from the garden or investing in some interesting varieties from the florist. If you buy from a florist, choose flowers that have the look of home-grown favorites, such as stocks, irises, snapdragons, gladiolus, and lilies. Much of a florists' traditional stock suffers from overuse—red rosebuds, white baby's breath, and pink carnations are dead giveaways that you've been to the flower shop and selected your blooms from the front of the case! Look a little further for flowers that will give your arrangement a truly distinctive air.

Here at Cedaridge Farm we enjoy giving harvest parties. All the leaves are added to the dining table, which is set up as a buffet, and we create a bountiful arrangement that highlights the harvest we celebrate. At Thanksgiving, we enjoy choosing a big pumpkin to hollow out for a "vase"; then we set about gathering the best blossoms, seedpods, and berries from the cutting garden and local hedgerows and fill the hollowed squash to overflowing. Fresh-baked pies and cakes and hot mulled cider are laid out for friends and family to enjoy.

The Kitchen and Bath

We love to add flowers to the bathroom and kitchen, where they can be admired as we go about our busy lives. Interior design magazines often show dramatic floral arrangements in these rooms, but the designers tend to use displays that were composed in a studio room and are impractical and out of character for our own homes. On our ritual evening walks through the gardens at Cedaridge Farm, we pick assorted blossoms that catch our eye because of their size or color, or because they are the first or last blooms of the season, and place them in the myriad small vases we have collected over the years.

These little gatherings are tucked into the oddest places—in the bathroom by the toothbrush holder, on the crowded window ledge above the kitchen sink. They are there for us to enjoy, providing unexpected pleasure throughout the day. Our other favorite surprising locations for some cheerful petals are beside the telephone, tucked into a bookcase, and next to our pillows—here we like to use fragrant flowers like lavender and chamomile that make us feel as though we are waking up in a field of wildflowers each morning.

The Bedroom

More than any other room in the house, the bedroom benefits from the freshness that flowers bring to an interior. Each of the arrangements in the different bedrooms of our farmhouse features a different style or color theme. The wallpaper with a delicate lavender and rose motif in one room is the perfect setting for a vase of tiny pink 'The Fairy' roses. The fireplace mantel in another bedroom offers the perfect location for a row of pots filled with large-flowered deep crimson zinnias. In autumn the zinnias are replaced with a basket of russet and yellow chrysanthemums surrounded with pine cones and moss. A small vanity table in our guest bedroom is an ideal spot for a simple bouquet of spring daffodils or garden roses, carefully positioned to reflect in the mirror.

Dried flowers can also be an asset in bedrooms; they add beauty and color while eliminating some of the daily care required to keep fresh flowers beautiful. At Cedaridge Farm every bedroom features some form of dried flowers—a wreath adorns a headboard, a container filled with tall arching grasses enlivens a corner, or dried garden flowers decorate the top of a dresser.

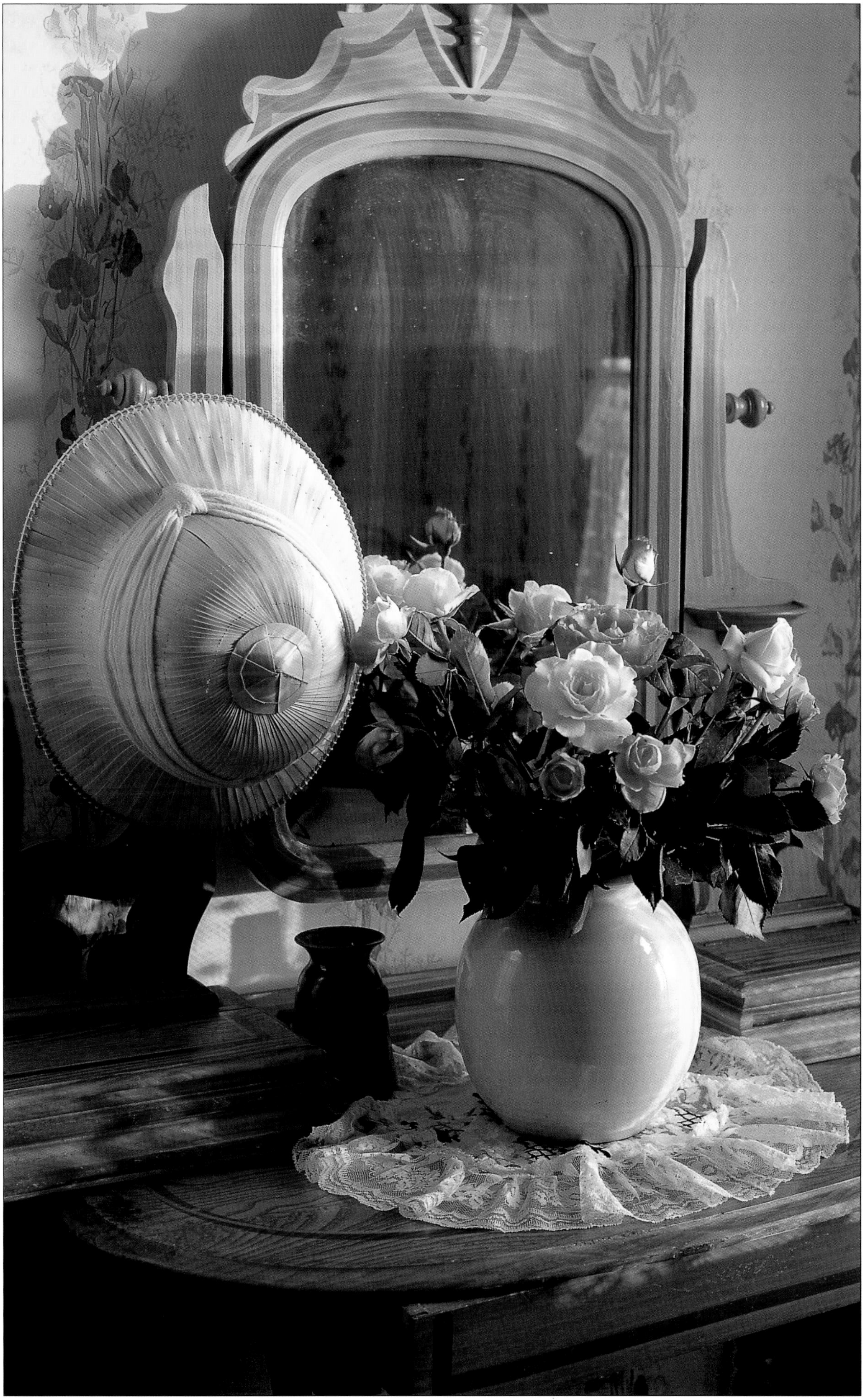

We encourage our children to gather flowers for their own rooms, giving them the freedom to choose the blossoms, foliage, and fruits they want. Even as we provide the children with this means for creative expression, we are instilling in them a love for living with flowers.

The Sunroom, Gazebo, and Garden

In selecting photographs for this book, we have chosen to display a number of examples in outdoor settings—in the gazebo, in the midst of our cutting garden, on the balcony—because the use of floral arrangements outdoors seems to have been almost overlooked in other books. Also, we find that natural light renders colors more faithfully than artificial indoor light.

Most importantly, we have chosen to show many examples in our bright sunroom—a Victorian-style conservatory—which we use more than any other room in the house. It is never without a fresh floral bouquet no matter what the season. It thrills us most when a thunderstorm or snowstorm rages outside, while inside we are blessed with comfort and fresh flowers! Our conservatory's natural ambience makes it the perfect setting for massive arrangements that can overpower other rooms. A recent addition to our farmhouse, we consider it the best investment we ever made.

Our second-best investment was a balcony off a raised back porch, with a sitting space to enjoy afternoon tea and watch the sun set over the garden. The white wicker table set between matching chairs is always resplendent with fresh flowers from the garden.

Both these locations are important to our use of flowers at home, but the gardens themselves yield a multitude of locations for our floral expression. We feel that our home and surroundings are unique and find that visitors appreciate its distinctive character even more when floral arrangements are in evidence both inside and outside the house. Special events at Cedaridge Farm—like weddings and open days for the garden—are made all the more extraordinary by cut flowers creatively arranged and strategically placed.

SOME GENERAL ADVICE ON PLACEMENT

Most old houses have deep window ledges, which are perfect locations for displaying flowers, especially old-fashioned flowers like peonies and hydrangeas. We always have a bouquet of the freshest flowers from the garden on display, but only on the window ledges that are protected from direct sun either by the trees outside or by a lace curtain against the window pane. Avoid placing flowers in direct sun, which causes fresh flowers to mature too quickly and dried flowers to be bleached of color.

Within rooms, look for spaces that will most beautifully harbor floral decorations, such as mantelpieces or tables below paintings. We use small antique Korean medicine chests to hold opulent bouquets; narrow, sturdy, and low, these lacquered wooden stands do not protrude uncomfortably into the room and thus reduce the risk of accidents.

Arrangements placed before mirrors offer another interesting opportunity for creative display. If you plan to site your flowers in front of a mirror, keep arrangements loose to take advantage of the added dimension offered by the reflection.

Flowers in any location should look as if they have just been put in place. Make sure to remove them before they begin to wither—they should be remembered at the height of their glory, not as they wane. Even dried flowers will look better when they are moved to a different space occasionally. If you have a location that is particularly good for an arrangement, use the space continuously, rotating between fresh and dried flowers.

FLOWERS FOR SPECIAL EVENTS

Although flowers bring cheer to every day of our lives, it is at the celebration of a special event that we seem to enjoy them most. Festive occasions let us bring out our best, from elegant vases to extravagant flower combinations.

Weddings

Nothing is more exciting than planning a wedding. Whether the wedding will be held indoors or out, it is a perfect opportunity to gather together the most beautiful flowers available and to present them in the most extravagant and creative way possible. Planned well in advance, the garden can be transformed into a dreamy landscape for a wedding. Arbors covered with roses, urns dripping with fuchsias, and baskets overflowing with annuals can make a memorable day truly unforgettable.

A garden wedding requires many months of planning. Hundreds of pansies, foxgloves, and delphiniums surround the bridal path leading to the Victorian gazebo where the service will be conducted. Small, fussy arrangements are lost in a open garden. Plan for big spreads of color instead. Guests will be seated in the shade of a spreading maple tree with a full view of the bride walking toward the gazebo.

*The entrance doors of
the church are decked
with bouquets that repeat
some of the blooms used
in the pew decorations.
Flowers include crimson
asters, purple stocks,
pink snapdragons, green
hydrangeas, and carol
garden roses accentuated
with Queen Anne's
lace.*

How beautiful a May wedding can be when inspiration is drawn from the Flemish Masters—fiery parrot tulips, pink cherry blossoms, blue Dutch irises, and pink bleeding hearts are a combination beloved by these painters, and with the flowers' pink, white, and blue tints, this combination is especially lovely for a spring wedding! A Victorian-style summer wedding is unforgettable when old-fashioned cottage garden flowers—tall pink foxgloves, powder blue delphiniums, creamy white peonies, bearded irises, pastel Canterbury bells, antique roses, and fragrant lavender—recall the beauty and romance of the Gilded Age.

Let deep colors assert their brilliance for a September wedding—crimson asters, purple stocks, rose pink snapdragons, green hydrangeas, and coral garden roses reflect the splendor of the season. Drape garlands of asparagus fern and tiny star-shaped sweet autumn clematis over balconies or backs of chairs.

Top: A close-up of this bridal bouquet reveals blue delphiniums, pink peonies, pink and white canterbury bells, blue lavender, and a deep pink old garden rose. These flowers were cut from the garden a few days before the wedding, properly conditioned, and arranged into a bouquet the morning of the wedding.

Bottom: Fan-shaped sprays at the end of the pews create a corridor of flowers.

Stun guests at a winter wedding with the passion of red and green. Decorate with armloads of evergreen branches, such as juniper, pine, and rhododendron, punctuated by avalanches of scarlet and crimson berries from holly, firethorn, crabapple, and winterberry bushes.

Christmas

The holidays are a special time at Cedaridge Farm. Yards and yards of garlands made with Scotch pine, blue spruce, and dusky blue berry-laden juniper are draped from beam to beam in every room. Bright red winterberry, orange bittersweet, and yellow crabapple branches; pink-flushed lady apples; fat pine cones; dried thistle, fern fronds, and milkweed and iris pods; and tiny white lights are threaded throughout the garlands. The fireplace mantels have a new motif every year, and we usually choose a theme based on nature. One year a beautiful white

Top: The house's entrance is decorated with a traditional evergreen wreath on the door; a still-life arrangement beside the door offers a pineapple—a traditional symbol of welcome—as a focal point. Bottom: This antique sleigh is the largest container we use for arrangements at Cedaridge Farm. Pulled out of the barn every Christmas, the sleigh is filled with holly berries and evergreens to create a festive seasonal display.

The eaves of a shingled roof display a garland composed of seasonal materials. The Christmas decoration includes apples, pomegranates, grapefruits, lemons, and pinecones attached to spruce and cypress evergreen boughs. Similar garlands are looped along the railings of the balcony and the conservatory's exterior.

wooden swan, nesting in an enormous gathering of dried sweet Annie, was the central figure. Flanking birch bark–covered containers held forced paperwhites and white poinsettias. A profusion of white roses tied with a raffia ribbon lay beside the swan to dry in place.

Another year, three old metal watering cans (one of them green) stood guard among a multitude of red poinsettias surrounded by pots of maiden hair ferns and evergreen boughs. Gold-painted iris pods shot out on all sides like rays of light. Yet another year, our purple martin birdhouse stood to one side, with forced forsythia branches—draped with tiny lights and long vines of ivy—creating a backdrop. Our collection of wooden and ceramic birds nestled among dried white oak leaves, white statice, plump brown pine cones, red apples, lime green osage oranges, and hardy yellow citrus fruits.

In addition to trimming the Scotch pine from our own grove, we "build" a leafless deciduous tree for the sitting room, using contorted twigs and branches saved throughout the year. The best branches are positioned together to make the "tree," from which we hang special ornaments made from seedpods and nuts gathered earlier in the autumn.

Our outdoor spaces are not forgotten during the holidays. Fresh wreaths are made and hung on doors, garden gates, and the side of the barn. The Victorian gazebo houses a Christmas tree all its own, covered with red ribbons and suet for the birds. Our antique sled is pulled from the barn and draped with pine, holly, and decorative berries, ever more beautiful when dusted lightly with snow.

Arrangi

Flowers Naturally

"Spring is tender green shoots and pink apple blossoms, Autumn is the contrast of yellow leaves against violet tones. If summer is the opposition of blues against an element of orange in the gold bronze of the corn, one could paint a picture which expressed the mood of the seasons in each of the contrasts of the complementary colors— red and green, blue and orange, yellow and violet, white and black."

Vincent van Gogh

in a letter to his brother Theo

Pictured here is a beautiful natural arrangement of summer-flowering annuals—including sunflowers, cosmos, zinnias, and blue sage—which echo the garden beyond. A small basket of nasturtiums, asters, and gloriosa daisies mirror the colors of the bouquet.

We borrow many of our ideas for arrangements from tried-and-true garden themes. This jumble of blooms—including dianthus, lady's mantle, chrysanthemums, delphiniums, lupines, and phlox—is reminiscent of an old-fashioned English cottage garden.

Any arrangement of flowers is inherently "un-natural," because in nature flowers do not grow in containers of water. However, there are ways to present flowers so that they look less contrived. Informal arrangements are the most natural, and they will look even more so if you use flowers in their appropriate season, echoing groupings that can be seen in the garden or during a stroll through the nearby countryside.

We love to visit our friend Olive Dunn in New Zealand, because after a stroll through her glittering garden we move indoors for tea and scones, every room of the house displaying the flowers we have just observed outdoors. Of course, this is no different from the way we welcome visitors to our own home, but everyone's garden and taste for flowers is different, reflecting highly personal creative energies. To see this principle executed so well in another setting is immensely pleasurable. Before retiring, Olive was a professional florist, and for many years she opened her garden to visitors. But no matter how uplifting the garden, the biggest thrill was to be invited indoors, through her sun porch, to see the bounty of the garden displayed in such ingenious ways—making use not only of picture-perfect dahlias, larkspurs, and gladiolus but also fruits and vegetables, foliage, and woody plants.

As a result of observing our reaction to other people's arrangements, we have become more aware of the importance of arranging flowers in a relaxed manner. This not only involves arranging the flowers in a more carefree, less stilted way but also affects the choice of plant material.

We spend hours each January with catalogs, seeking unusual vegetables to grow for visual interest, varieties like 'Rainbow' chard and 'Annie Oakley' okra. Dried corn tassels are gathered to add texture to late summer bouquets, and even curly green bunches of parsley can enliven arrangements with a richness of green unmatched in the plant kingdom. The "naturalness" of garden-raised fruits and vegetables is so alluring that we have found that visitors are often more impressed with arrangements that incorporate these than they are by arrangements that use only flowers. People tend to linger over these unusual displays and are always inquisitive about the particular varieties featured.

Our herb garden has become an important source of material for natural-looking arrangements. Many herbs actually improve with age. Not only do their aromas and flavors intensify, their stems and stalks often dry into interesting shapes and textures. The subtle yellow-green flower heads of dill, for example, radiate like the spokes of a wheel. These are easily dried to add a starburst effect in arrangements. Chocolate mint, another hardy perennial, has lustrous dark green foliage with chocolate-colored stems. In summer the plant produces colorful pink flower spikes that last well in water. As it dries, the chocolate-peppermint aroma intensifies, making a refreshing tea and a valuable aromatic ingredient for potpourris.

The onion family is rich in plants for our herb gardens, especially common pink, spring-flowering chives and white, summer-flowering Chinese chives. The spent flowers of both form

brittle, dome-shaped seedpods, which are easily stored for dried arrangements and can be used to break up the too-formal lines of many cut flowers.

Ornamental grasses are also incredibly successful at making arrangements look natural and can be used either alone in an all-grass arrangement or combined with flowers to bring a softness and soothing elegance to the display.

Although we have an ornamental grass garden at Cedaridge Farm, we also tuck clumps of grasses into our perennial beds, which make the beds look more natural and provide us with plenty of leaves and flower plumes for our arrangements. Along the banks of our stream, the slender leaves of grasses are allowed to bend forward and dip their tips into the water. We are especially fond of the soft, bottlebrush flower spikes of pink fountain grass and the white, featherlike blooms of 'Silver Feather' eulalia grass. Pampas plume is somewhat overused in flower arrangements because it is so widely available through florists, and we find that the common pampas plume available from California growers tends to be large and overpowering. We do like, however, the new dwarf variety 'Pumila', not only because the plumes are not as big, but also because the plant is hardy enough to overwinter in our Pennsylvania garden. A single plant can produce fifty plumes.

Two favorite grasses that originated in Europe are northern sea oats (which have rich brown pendant seed clusters) and the fluffy white annual hare's tail grass, which we have admired along cliffs in Brittany and New Zealand's Bay of Plenty. Both of these easy-to-grow grasses last forever in dried arrangements, though we wince whenever we see the hare's tail dyed unnatural gaudy colors. Many ornamental grasses look perfectly natural when used alone, but some spectacular arrangements can be made by combining an assortment of different grass plumes. Also, the stiffness of many floral arrangements can be softened considerably by the judicious addition of grasses, particularly those with pendant seed heads, such as Job's tears, sea oats, and Indian rice.

Often pushing through the snow, cup-shaped Lenten roses are the first flowers to bloom at Cedaridge Farm. Their stunning color makes them an irresistible flower for cutting.

MAKING THE MOST OF THE SEASON

The main contents for an arrangement are often an expression of the season, for good seasonal content inspires the most dramatic displays. By knowing when flowers come into season—and their life cycles—it is possible to enjoy gorgeous bouquets throughout the entire year.

At Cedaridge Farm, we note the beginning of each flowering season as early blooming Lenten roses appear. We begin gathering these spotted, cup-shaped, nodding flowers in February, just as the last of our winterberry, holly, and dried fountain grasses are used up. The leathery evergreen leaves and porcelainlike petals make uplifting bouquets when it seems like winter will never loosen its grip. From white through pink to maroon, the delicate flowers last in the garden well into May, drying to shades of green and cream. April brings us thousands of daffodils in a multitude of varieties. Some of our favorites for gathering are 'Professor Einstein', for its wide, flat, frilly, orange-red cup; 'Pink Charm', for its intense pink trumpet; and the giant 'Fortissimo', an orange and yellow bicolor. Every room in our farmhouse is filled with bright, fragrant blossoms picked fresh every morning. Often, we place duets of forsythia and daffodils on the windowsill for a dramatic yellow display. Tulips in a rainbow of colors begin to weave their magic throughout the gardens in early May, while pink dogwoods, coral quince, old-fashioned lilacs, lavender azaleas, and magenta redbuds are skirted by a haze of blue from the delicate blossoms of grape hyacinths, forget-me-nots, and Spanish bluebells. Weeping cherry tree limbs droop to the ground with their delightfully delicate pale pink blossoms, and winter pansies lift their cheerful faces everywhere.

A heavy concrete garden urn on a balustrade is filled with hot-colored summer-flowering daylilies and red bee balm, echoing the beauty of the garden beyond.

By early summer, our cottage garden is overflowing with sky blue columbine, shell pink lupines, purple spotted foxgloves, fragrant sweet Williams, old-fashioned sweet peas, billowing pink peonies, snow white feverfew, satiny poppies, vining star-shaped clematis, and red, white, and blue larkspur, all mingling with a multitude of old-fashioned roses. Ox-eye daisies, a prolific wildflower, dance in the fields and are gathered daily to use as fill for all our arrangements. The wild multiflora rose is an important base-fill flower for arrangements in June, as one good branch fills a container in a frothy display. Some sprigs of chartreuse lady's mantle blossoms will serve the same purpose. Twigs encrusted with lichen, sinuous vines studded with mint green leaves, bark peeled from our groves of river birch, and cushions of soft moss are gathered all summer long to add drama and interest to the arrangements of garden flowers. Fox-tail grasses and timothy heads are cut from the meadow to use fresh or are bunched together, tied, and hung upside down to dry for use in future arrangements.

By the middle of summer, the cutting garden yields bountiful baskets of all our favorite old-fashioned, easy-to-grow annual flowers, including cosmos, cornflowers, zinnias, snapdragons, marigolds, salvia, and stocks. Nearby, the perennial borders yield armloads of pink and blue bearded irises, yarrow in yellow and pastel shades, bright red Maltese cross, and masses of purple coneflowers. By midsummer, the meadow is filled with the ephemeral beauty of Queen Anne's lace. Cut on a daily basis, this flower will last for several weeks when properly conditioned. It continues to bloom in the field until the end of September in the company of blue chicory, a delicate, blue, star-shaped flower that blooms only in the morning. Daylilies, gladiolus, asters, sweet autumn clematis, stocks, and dahlias bloom in profusion.

In our quest for a more natural look, we search beyond the confines of our cultivated garden for unusual content. We scour the local woodlands for orange and gray lichen-covered branches and cushions of green moss, and we search the hedgerows for bramble canes laden with blackberries, seed heads and pods of wildflowers, and wayside grasses. When we find a unique stone formation or a hollow piece of log, we seize on it as a more natural way to display a fern or alpine plant.

Even as the threat of frost lingers in the air, goldenrod turns the fields a brilliant yellow, accented by the blue of New England asters. The last of our blue and pink hydrangeas are harvested, but it is chrysanthemums that outshine all else in the garden, providing not only a lavish garden display but masses of russet-colored flowers for tabletops and windowsills. Dill and chocolate mint—from our herb garden—add texture and subtle color to our harvest bouquets. Seedpods of Siberian and Japanese irises are gathered now, along with ruby red rose hips. Orange-berried bittersweet and scarlet-leafed Virginia creeper are vines we gather from the hedgerow. The vegetable garden is also a rich source of late-season material; we especially like dried okra pods and gourds. Pumpkins are hollowed out to create containers for the harvest table. As frost tints the morning landscape, the last of the flowers from our cutting garden are picked for drying.

Even after the first frost, we stay busy gathering dry and woody material to use in our arrangements. Contorted twigs of hazel and branches from old apple, pear, and peach trees are now treasured, as are whips of yellow- and red-twig dogwoods, which we store undercover in big cardboard boxes. The brilliant yellow, red, and scarlet leaves of sugar maples are collected, carefully placed between the pages of old telephone books, and put aside for winter pressed-flower projects. Walks through the woods yield a multitude of decorative nuts and pine cones. Nubby lime green fruits of the osage orange, fragrant fruits of hardy citrus, and lemon-scented green-skinned black walnut hulls are gathered to make hanging ornaments and cone-shaped ornamental trees for the holidays. But most uplifting of all is the bounty of berries we cut and use well into winter—winterberries, hollies, beauty berries, cotoneaster, viburnums, pyracantha, and crabapples, with colors that range from yellow through orange to scarlet, crimson, and deep purple—all planted in a special berry garden. Wild pokeweed and elderberry shrub are encouraged to grow here, adding to the variety of berries for harvesting. We also like these plants for the birds they draw, and we enjoy their song as we gather our branches from this natural habitat.

Carolyn has created an appropriate harvest festival arrangement using flowers, fruits, and vegetables gathered from our autumn garden. A large pumpkin holds vines of morning glory and Chinese lantern, which have been twined through hydrangeas, dill, milkweed pods, and Indian corn. The edibles—cheeses and freshly baked apple pies—are perfect accompaniments to this seasonal design.

A familiar sight at

Cedaridge Farm—

buckets of flowers stand

ready for arranging.

FLOWERS FROM THE FLORIST
AND GARDEN CENTER

Weekly visits to the local garden center yield the extra flowers we need to complete special arrangements. Rather than buying a dozen tightly budded red roses from a florist, we prefer to purchase an entire rosebush from the garden center. Once we have cut the blossoms we need, we plant the bush in the garden so that it can rejuvenate and provide future enjoyment. Potted bulbs, small flowering shrubs, perennials, annuals, and vegetables are all worth buying when you want a special color or shape for an arrangement.

Making friends with the local florist is important. Often, when the perfect flower is missing from the garden, it can be ordered and shipped overnight to meet a tight deadline. Although we prefer not to mix flowers that are out of season, it is sometimes advantageous to see what the florist has in the cooler that might complement flowers cut from your garden. One Asiatic lily or a few Dutch irises might be the perfect addition to an otherwise sparse arrangement of garden blossoms. The only plants we try to avoid are the expensive tropical ones—anthuriums, gingers, and proteas—which are too exotic and ostentatious for our taste and rarely mix well with our own cut flowers. We think they look sensational in museum foyers and hotel lobbies but out of place in a Pennsylvania farmhouse and, indeed, in most homes.

Florists have varying preferences for the flowers they keep in the cooler. We learned this the hard way when we were putting the finishing touches on twelve centerpieces for a luncheon at the local art league and wanted to add a splash of yellow to the small blue-and-pink cottage garden arrangements we were making. The perfect choice was a tiny yellow clustered *Solidaster* (often referred to as yellow aster), which is a common filler flower and is usually available at a florist's shop. We called five florists before finding the few small sprigs that we needed! It is also important to learn the life cycle of cut flowers so that you know you are buying the freshest flowers. As flowers mature, the pollen becomes loose or fluffy, often falling from the flower, a good indication that it is too old to offer long vase life. The flower head of a fresh flower is firm, and the leaves are lustrous.

DRYING FLOWERS

A benefit of many popular fresh flowers is that they can be dried effectively, extending their life beyond the fresh state. Most flowers will dry beautifully simply hung upside down in a dark, dry, well-ventilated, warm place. This form of air drying is especially effective for drying airy sprays like gypsophila and tapering sprays like larkspur. Many flowers have a natural tendency to dry on the plant and require very little additional drying treatment. These flowers have papery petals and are known as everlastings. They include statice, strawflowers, immortelle, starflower, pearly everlasting, and globe amaranth. Another group of everlastings is grown for its parchmentlike seed cases. We would never be without silvery money plant or reddish-orange Chinese lanterns, which look perfectly natural bunched together in a vase.

A few years ago, while studying the works of the French Impressionist painters, we visited the studio of Cézanne, located in his home in Aix-en-Provence. Upon entering the foyer, we were entranced by the spicy fragrance of dried herbs and flowers. We instantly felt that we were enter-

Dried flowers, preserved throughout the growing season, remind us of many pleasurable hours spent in the garden. Here, their soft golden glow echoes the colors of advancing autumn beyond the window panes.

113

ARRANGING
FLOWERS
NATURALLY

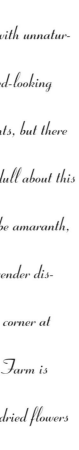
Dried flowers are often associated with unnatural and faded-looking arrangements, but there is nothing dull about this statice, globe amaranth, and sea lavender display. This corner at Cedaridge Farm is filled with dried flowers throughout the year.

ing a very special place, the home of a person who obviously loved nature. Stems of dried dill stood in large crocks and hung from the ceiling. Tied bunches of sweet Annie, anise, lavender, and dried roses completely covered the ceiling over a dark narrow winding stairway that led to the large studio. We immediately decided our home should always have a natural, comforting, unforgettable fragrance, and we began to use these same fragrant dried herbs in similar ways.

Valerie Ford, president of the National Association of Flower Arrangement Societies of Great Britain, recently advocated a greater tolerance of experimentation with different styles to ensure that the flower arranging movement continues to evolve. "Arranging flowers is an art form with parallels in painting and sculpture," she noted. "It is just as valid to make pictures or shapes from plant material as from oil paint. But if you do not seek to explore and extend the scope of your material, your work will become sterile and repetitious."

We concur with Ms. Ford; we may not always like all of the modern developments in our art, but if the arrangements are skillfully executed and explore the possibilities of form and texture with a fresh eye, then we shall all gain from a widening of our horizons and the stretching of our imaginations.

Most reassuring is the new attitude toward arranging flowers that has come with the expanded opportunities for learning in the form of books and videos. A giant step forward has come with the recognition of flower arranging as entertainment—audiences everywhere pay to learn from skilled flowers arrangers like Sheila McQueen and Barry Ferguson as they create spectacular flower arrangements before our eyes, sprinkling their talk with amusing anecdotes.

Once we have a clear understanding of how to handle structure, color, texture, clarity, harmony, and proportion, there is no limit to the scope of designs possible using plants as our palette. Indeed, the age of flower arranging is still very young, and opportunities for individuality of expression are infinite.

MAKING A WREATH OF DRIED FLOWERS

This gorgeous wreath is easy to make, and can be assembled at a fraction of its purchasing price at any home decor shop. Feel free to substitute your own favorites for the flowers and leaves used here, giving rein to all your creative impulses. Make your wreath as small and dainty or large and lush as you like.

MATERIALS:				
Hydrangea	Pink celosia	Red roses	Lamb's ears	18-gauge wire
Sweet Annie	Purple statice	Sea lavender	Wire wreath frame	Wire clippers

1 First, gather together all the materials you will need. This wreath is made with a wire frame (available at craft stores), flowers we have dried, and a few fresh leaves picked from our garden.

2 Cover the wreath frame with the sweet Annie, securing the flowers by wrapping the 18-gauge wire around the stems. Green wire is preferable because it blends well with plant leaves and stems.

3 Continue to wind wire around the form, adding stems of the various flowers and leaf stalks as you go.

4 Check to see that the wreath has a balanced but casual look. Adjust any flowers that seem out of place.

5 The finished wreath has a very delicate look that appears perfectly natural on this old side door.

A Cutting Garden

of Your Own

"This little island garden of mine is so small that

the amount of pure delight it gives in the course

of a summer is something hardly

to be credited."

Celia Thaxter,

An Island Garden

The harvest of daffodils in early spring brightens everything at Cedaridge Farm. Planted at the edges of the property, the daffodils come back every year. For longest lasting displays, daffodils can be cut in bud to open their flowers indoors.

The harvest of summer annuals includes pink zinnias, yellow and orange marigolds, crimson strawflowers, and yellow gloriosa daisies. The more these varieties are cut, the more the plants are stimulated into initiating new flowering buds.

Cutting gardens are intended as "farms" of a sort—farms that produce plenty of plants with long stems suitable for cutting. The best cutting gardens produce a continuous supply of annuals, perennials, roses, and flowering bulbs from spring through autumn, beginning with daffodils and finishing with dahlias and asters. Medium-size and tall flowering plants are best for cutting; however, a few shorter varieties, such as star zinnia, pansies, and forget-me-nots, can be as charming in an arrangement as in the garden. Flowering vines are also a vital addition because they are great space-savers—a single trellis allows several types of flowers to entwine their handsome colors.

Cutting gardens are best located in full sun because the preponderance of flowers suitable for cutting grow best in bright light. The area need not be large, but it should contain a wide variety of flowers in all shapes, colors, textures, and bloom sizes, giving a broad spectrum of choices for different types of arrangements.

ANNUALS

Annuals are essential flowers for a cutting garden. Many, such as zinnias, celosias, and cosmos, are "everblooming"; the more they are cut, the more the plants are stimulated into producing new flower stems. The same is true of the dahlia, a prolific-blooming summer-flowering bulb that will continue flowering on long stems until autumn frost.

At Cedaridge Farm, we grow annuals in an area separate from perennials and bulbs, mainly because the ground for annuals must be dug up and prepared anew each season, but the perennials and bulbs can be left in place. Our annual garden is in the shape of a square and is divided down the center by a flagstone path, with the rows running perpendicular to the path. The straight rows are two feet (61cm) wide, with a one-foot (30.5cm) walkway between each row, which provides easy access for cutting.

In the spring, we turn over the soil in the annual beds and add garden compost and a general purpose fertilizer. The parallel rows are then mounded in preparation for the new season.

The annuals are grown either from transplants or seeds, which are sown directly into the place where they are to grow. Plants like zinnias, poppies, cornflowers, and sunflowers germinate quickly and reliably from seed but others, such as snapdragons, larkspurs, celosias, and blue salvia, are best started indoors to gain healthy transplants. Often, when there are varieties we want to add to the garden but prefer to have only a few plants, it is most efficient to purchase plants in six-packs from the local garden center. Although we plant basically the same varieties from one year to the next, change their positions within the garden so that the design is never the same.

The lower level of the cutting garden at Cedaridge Farm primarily features perennials such as these spirelike foxgloves and silvery lamb's ears.

After frost has turned the stems brown, we pull the annuals up by their roots, shake the soil free, and deposit the debris in the compost pile. Then we turn over the soil, add some soil conditioner like peat or compost, and leave the garden fallow until spring, when it is ready to prepare for a new planting.

PERENNIALS

The perennial section of the cutting garden adjoins the annual garden. It also includes some bulb varieties, such as daffodils, gladiolus, and dahlias, and some biennials, such as foxgloves, sweet Williams, and Canterbury bells. The garden slopes downward, and the space is terraced to produce three separate planting levels. Some of the important perennials in this area include Shasta daisies, peonies, hostas, rudbeckias, bearded irises, and asters.

The perennial cutting garden requires that we clear old stems after frost in autumn. We burn these stems or relegate them to a compost pile. Each clump of perennials produces young plants, which can be separated, or divided, and planted in other parts of the garden. Although some perennials grow faster that others, each plant must be checked periodically to ensure that it has not become too invasive. If a particular specimen seems to have grown too big for its allotted space, dig it up and divide it, replanting the parent plant in the original spot.

In general, perennials are heavy feeders, so we try to fertilize twice a season—in autumn after frost has browned most of the stems and again in spring before the leaves break dormancy. If we have time to fertilize only once, then we do it in the autumn.

Many tall-growing perennials will need to be staked to prevent them from toppling over. These include English delphiniums, peonies, and most asters. We also like to stake gladiolus and dahlias to ensure long, straight stems.

A few flowering shrubs, including a lilac, butterfly bush, dogwood, and pussy willow, are strategically planted in the perennial garden. The garden is completely enclosed with a picket

fence, not only for ornamental value but because it allows a large collection of flowering perennial vines and climbing shrubs, such as old country roses, honeysuckle, and clematis. Having plants that grow *up* rather than *out* is extremely space-efficient. This fence is suffi-ciently long to accommodate a host of annual vines as well, notably morning glories, nastur-tiums, and sweet peas.

We've planned the beds in the perennial section to allow for massing plants together. Each space is planted in a diamond pattern because this avoids a regimented appearance. To allow access into the middle of these large beds, we place stepping stones at strategic intervals, which cushions the weight of our feet and keeps the soil from becoming compacted.

For a decorative touch, we've dressed the perennial garden with an arbor, which, together with the picket fence, makes it resemble an English cottage garden. These garden features are in perfect harmony with the Victorian-style gazebo, which sits at one end of the flagstone path that leads through the annual garden.

Although the primary purpose of these two spaces is to grow plants for cutting, the areas do double duty as beautiful display gardens. We have the best of both worlds—sensational outdoor spaces and armloads of cut flowers to decorate the inside of our home.

Following is a plan that shows how the two gardens are separate yet are connected in over-all design. The plant varieties listed are the ones we favor for the purpose of cutting.

This island bed of orange, yellow, and red Asiatic lilies, yellow glo-riosa, red bee balm, and hot pink miniature roses features a combination of annuals and perennials in a "hot" color harmony.

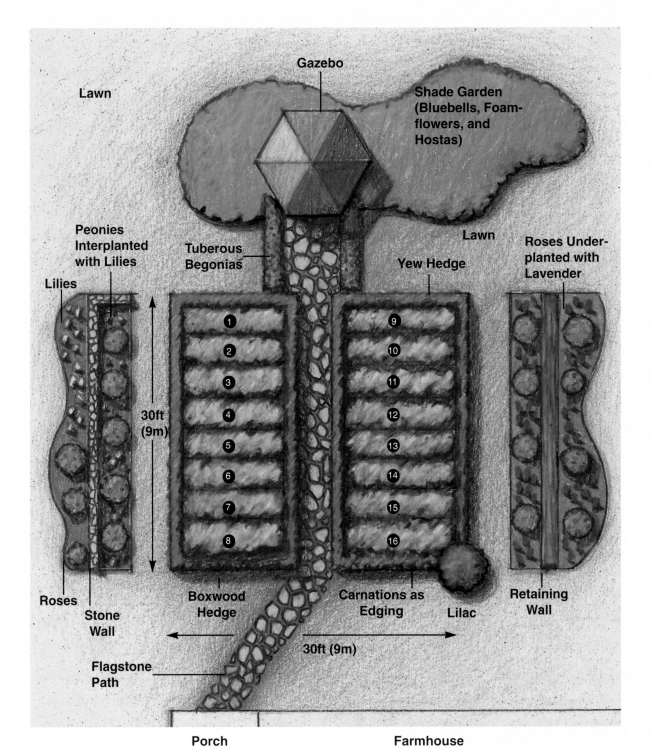

Gazebo

Lawn

Shade Garden
(Bluebells, Foam-
flowers, and
Hostas)

Lawn

Peonies
Interplanted
with Lilies

Tuberous
Begonias

Yew Hedge

Roses Under-
planted with
Lavender

Lilies

30ft
(9m)

30ft (9m)

Roses

Stone
Wall

Boxwood
Hedge

Carnations as
Edging

Lilac

Retaining
Wall

Flagstone
Path

Porch

Farmhouse

1. Foxgloves, Columbine, Money Plant
2. Calliopsis, Globe Amaranth
3. Blanket Flower, Rudbeckias
4. Cockscomb, Everlasting
5. Zinnias, Lady's Mantle
6. Snapdragons, Asters
7. Heliotrope, Marigolds
8. Chinese Forget-Me-Nots, Gladiolus

9. Cosmos
10. Sunflowers
11. Ageratum, Blue Salvia
12. Bells of Ireland, Cornflowers
13. Thoroughwax
14. Dahlias
15. Calendula, Pincushion Flower
16. Larkspur, Poppies

Ageratum, Flossflower (*Ageratum* spp.): 'Blue Horizon'

Aster (*Aster* spp.): 'Matsumoto Formula' series, 'Opus', and 'Giant Princess'

Bells of Ireland *(Molucella laevis)*

Blanket Flower (*Gaillardia* spp.)

Blue Salvia *(Salvia azurea)*: 'Victoria'

Calendula (*Calendula* spp.): 'Prince' mix

Calliopsis *(Coreopsis tinctoria)*

Chinese Forget-Me-Nots *(Cynoglossum amabile)*

Cockscomb *(Celosia cristata)*: 'Chief' mix and 'Flamingo Feather'

Columbine (*Aquilegia* spp.): 'Barlow' series and 'McKana Giant' mix

Cornflowers *(Centaurea cyanus)*: 'Florist Blue Boy'

Cosmos *(Cosmos bipinnatus)*: 'Sensation' series, 'Psyche', 'Candy Stripes', 'Versailles Carmine', and 'White Sonata'

Dahlias (*Dahlia* hybrids)

Everlasting, Immortelle *(Helichrysum)*: 'Mammoth-Flowered' series

Foxgloves *(Digitalis purpurea)*: 'Foxy' mix

Gladiolus (*Gladiolus* hybrids): 'Orchidiola'

Globe Amaranth *(Gomphrena globosa)*: 'Strawberry Fields' and 'Orange Globe'

Heliotrope *(Heliotropium)*: 'Marine'

Lady's Mantle *(Alchemilla)*: 'Thriller'

Larkspur *(Delphinium elatum)*: 'Giant Imperial' (individual colors)

Marigolds (*Tagetes* hybrids): 'Gold Coin' mix

Money Plant (*Lunaria* spp.)

Pincushion Flower *(Scabiosa)*: 'Blue Lace'

Poppies (*Papaver* spp.): 'Champagne Bubbles' Iceland poppy and 'Shirley Double' mix Shirley poppy

Rudbeckia, Black-eyed Susan, Gloriosa Daisy (*Rudbeckia* spp.): 'Indian Summer' black-eyed Susans and 'Rustic Colors' gloriosa daisies

Snapdragons *(Antirrhinum majus)*: 'Rocket' mix

Sunflowers (*Helianthus* hybrids): 'Italian White', 'Valentine', and 'Velvet Queen'

Thoroughwax *(Bupleurum)*: 'Green Gold'

Zinnias (*Zinnia* spp.): 'Ruffles' mix, 'Cut and Come Again', and 'State Fair' mix

123

A CUTTING GARDEN OF YOUR OWN

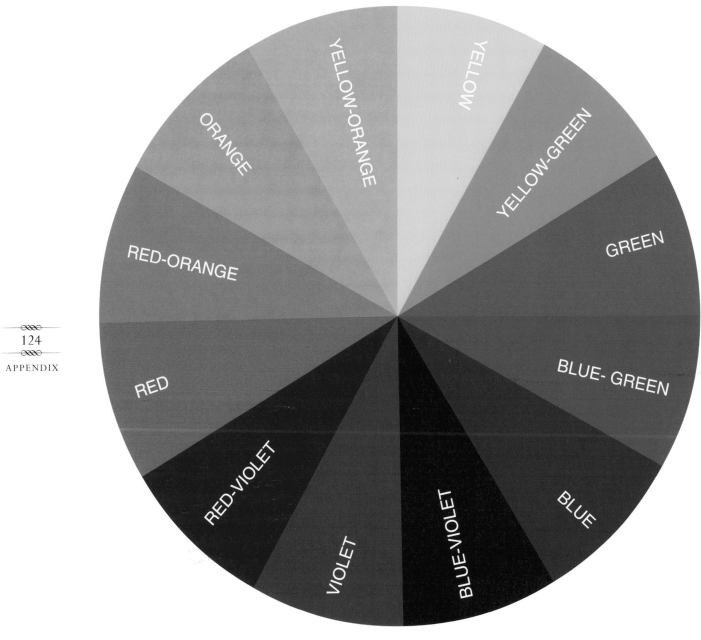

THE COLOR WHEEL

About the Authors

Derek Fell is a writer and photographer who specializes in garden design. He and his wife, Carolyn, live in Bucks County, Pennsylvania, at historic Cedaridge Farm, Tinicum Township, where they cultivate extensive award-winning flower and vegetable gardens that have been featured in *Architectural Digest, Hemispheres, Gardens Illustrated, Beautiful Gardens, Fine Gardening, American Nurseryman, Birds and Blooms,* and *Mid-Atlantic Country* magazines. Born and educated in England, Derek moved to Pennsylvania in 1964 to work for Burpee Seeds as their catalog manager, later taking on duties as executive director of the All-America Selections (the national seed trials) and the National Garden Bureau (an information office sponsored by the American seed industry). Now the author of more than fifty garden books and calendars, he has traveled widely, documenting gardens in North America, Europe, Africa, New Zealand, and Asia. His most recent books are *Perennial Gardening with Derek Fell* (Friedman/Fairfax), *Vegetable Gardening with Derek Fell* (Friedman/Fairfax), *Renoir's Garden* (Simon & Schuster), and *The Impressionist Garden* (Simon & Schuster). Derek's latest project is entitled *The Secrets of Monet's Garden.* He also worked as a consultant on gardening to the White House during the Ford Administration.

Derek is the winner of more awards from the Garden Writers Association of America than any other garden writer. Wall calendars, greeting cards, and art posters featuring his photography are published worldwide. Derek's photo art poster, *Monet's Bridge,* is sold at the Monet Museum in Giverny. He has lectured at numerous art museums, including the Smithsonian Institution in Washington, D.C.; the Philadelphia Museum of Art, the Barnes Foundation, Philadelphia; and the Denver Art Museum, Colorado. He is also host of the popular garden show for the QVC cable television shopping channel entitled *Step-by-Step Gardening,* which reaches an audience of more than fifty million homes.

Carolyn Fell is a professional design consultant who specializes in floral design and color harmonies. After a brief period as a congressional aide in Washington, D.C., she graduated from Parson's School of Design in New York and traveled the world for fifteen years as a specialist in color and new product design for leading fashion designers, including Pierre Cardin and Calvin Klein.

Since 1985 Carolyn has focused on flower arranging, highlighting the use of color inspired by the great French Impressionist painters. Her work as a stylist has been published in numerous calendars, catalogs, and books, including *Growing and Arranging Flowers* (Friedman/Fairfax), *Cutting Gardens* (Simon & Schuster), and *Flower Arranging with Perennials* (Spring Hill Nurseries). She is also set designer for the successful *Step-by-Step Gardening* show, seen on the QVC cable television shopping channel.

Carolyn is a frequent lecturer at regional events, such as "Art in Bloom" at the Walters Art Gallery in Baltimore, Maryland, and "The Southern Garden Symposium" in Fayetteville, Arkansas. In addition, she conducts flower arranging workshops at Cedaridge Farm and local garden clubs. Carolyn maintains a list of private clients, supplying arrangements for weddings and other special events.

SOURCES

Following are some of our favorite sources for seeds, plants, containers, and supplies.

UNITED STATES

Dorothy Biddle Service
  U.S. Route 6
  Greeley, PA 18425
  Fine selection of flower arranging supplies, including pinholders, clippers, snippers, floral tapes, and more.

George W. Park Seed Co., Inc.
  Cokesbury Road
  Greenwood, SC 29647-0001
  Good variety of seeds for both annuals and perennials.

Johnny's Selected Seeds
  Foss Hill Road
  Albion, ME 04190-0731
  Offers the latest varieties for cutting, along with good color and plant performance information.

Kinsman Company, Inc.
  River Road
  Point Pleasant, PA 18950
  Great selection of beautiful and unusual Victorian wirework baskets, hanging chandelier baskets, flower baskets with handles, and many other items useful as containers, including decorative clay pottery and French florists' vases. Supplier of cages for fresh flower chains (excellent for constructing wreaths, garlands, and swags with fresh flowers).

Klehm Nursery
  Route 5, Box 197
  South Barrington, IL 60010
  Outstanding source for herbaceous peonies and tree peonies, plus an extensive listing of daylilies.

Kurt Bluemel Inc.
  2740 Green Lane
  Baldwin, MD 31013
  Good source of grasses to use for drying.

Schreiner's
  36662 Quinaby Road, NE
  Salem, OR 97303-9720
  Excellent source of the latest varieties and colors of irises.

Shepherd's Garden Seeds
  Order Department
  30 Irene Street
  Torrington, CT 06790-6658
  Source for old-fashioned varieties for the cutting garden. Catalog gives full information for every variety.

Spring Hill Nurseries
  6523 North Galena Road
  Peoria, IL
  Excellent source for a wide variety of high-quality perennials and roses.

Stokes Seeds, Inc.
  Box 548
  Buffalo, NY 14240-0548
  Great choices of flowers by individual color, with excellent information on good cutting varieties.

CANADIAN SOURCES

Aimers
  81 Temperence Street
  Aurora, Ontario
  L4G 2R1

Ferncliff Gardens
  SS1
  Mission, British Columbia
  V2V 5V6

McFayden Seed Co. Ltd.
  Box 1800
  Brandon, Manitoba
  R7A 6N4

Rawlinson Garden Seed
  269 College Road
  Truro, Nova Scotia
  B2N 2P6

128